Catholic
Traditions
in the
Garden

Catholic Traditions in the Garden

Ann Ball

Our Sunday Visitor Publishing Division
Our Sunday Visitor, Inc.
Huntington, Indiana 46750

This one is for my Papa, one of the world's gentle souls, who always had time to talk to me about nature, and who somehow led me to see the living God in His creation. It's for Chuck, who loves trees; for Randy, whose thumb is more green than mine; and for my grandchildren, from "Oma Bruja."

Contents
and List of Projects

The Pope Speaks on Nature

After three days of rest and walks in the mountainous area of his Alpine retreat in northern Italy, Pope John Paul II spoke to several hundred people during his Sunday blessing and talk on July 14, 1996.

Calling for human beings to establish a more respectful relationship with nature, the pope said, "Increasingly aware of the value of the cosmos, we are stimulated to meditate on the seriousness of so many profanations of the environment, often perpetrated with unacceptable thoughtlessness."

He continued his remarks by pointing out that many people today are fascinated by "false myths" and thus lose sight of the richness of the created world, which can inspire strong spiritual sentiments.

A Prayer

Almighty and ever-living God, in the midst of the busyness of daily life, let me pause for a quiet moment to notice the architecture of a seashell, the perfume of a flower, the color of a leaf, or the warmth of an animal. Help me to see Your beauty and love in all of creation. Let me remember that You have given the earth and its fulness to mankind, and help me to be a good steward of Your gifts as I wait in faith and hope in this world to see You in the next. Amen.

Introduction (and Advice!)

What this book is not

This book is not in any way a standard gardening book. If you want to know an annual from a perennial, the difference between a root and a rhizome, or what constitutes a good fertilizer, you will have to look elsewhere. This book will not tell you how to grow a bigger tomato, nor will it tell you how to control pesky garden pests.

What this book is

This is a book about Catholic traditions and a book to help celebrate and use God's natural gifts to man.

Today, in our industrialized society, we are often so pressed for time that we do not "take time to smell the roses." City dwellers often have only a glimpse of green in their daily rush to and from work, although many draw a bit of nature into their lives via houseplants, cut flowers, and pets, while others work hard to maintain manicured lawns or small gardens. Many Americans living in rural areas have a better opportunity to experience the beauties of nature, but they, too, often find the daily pressures of life wearying. One lonely little book can't change that.

Then what, and why, is this book?

The Catholic Church is global. Throughout its history there are strands of many traditions, including those that celebrate nature. The people of the Church come from many cultures; each of these cultures contributes to the beauty of our living Faith. In today's busy world, a look at some of these traditions can provide a way to draw our Faith into our daily lives. This book can serve as a brief "time out" to help the reader recall the beauties of God's creation.

This is also a book to use. The projects are structured to be easy for those with "green thumbs" and "black thumbs" alike. Simplicity of construction and time constraints were prime requirements for inclusion, and projects were designed to include every member of the family. Projects included are suitable for individuals, but many will work as well for groups.

I grew up in an agricultural area. When I finished high school, I became a city dweller. There is an old saying that you can "take the girl out of the country but you can't take the country out of the girl." This was certainly apt in my case, and I have maintained a lifelong love affair with the things of nature.

I have poignant memories of my days as a young bride when we moved to a state far from home where we didn't know anyone. Everything was strange and different. The city was congested, we had a tiny apartment with no grass, and even the trees were unfamiliar.

One morning after my husband left for work, I began to walk, feeling lonely and homesick, through the dismal neighborhood of concrete and apartments. After blocks that seemed like miles, I turned a corner and discovered a house surrounded by a beautiful garden that was like a fairyland with its riot of flowers. Here were lilies and roses, zinnias and sweet peas, gladioli and marigolds! Flowers really did grow in California!

As I stood by the fence with tears streaming down my face, the lady of the house walked out and spoke to me. I blurted out my homesickness, and told her how beautiful her garden was all in one sentence. It turned out that her daughter was away at college in my home state. After a brief visit, I left with an armful of flowers and a fresh outlook on my new home. I have long forgotten the lady's name; I will never forget her kindness, or the lessons God taught me with the consoling beauty of that lady's flowers.

"There is no unbelief. / Whoever sees 'neath the field of winter snow / The silent harvest of the future grow, / God's Power must know" (Edward Bulwer-Lytton).

May you enjoy your "time out," reading about and celebrating the glories of God's creation through our Catholic traditions.

Tool Talk

Most of the materials and supplies used in the projects in this book should be readily available throughout the United States. I have included some addresses of mail order sources see page 154), but part of the fun of making things is finding the best and cheapest place to buy the supplies. Throughout the text I will include hints on places to look for supplies.

In this book, I have tried to include projects that do not call for exotic or expensive tools. Here are some things you'll need:

- A basic set of acrylic paints
- A jar of gesso prepping plaster (obtain from an art supplies or crafts store)
- A hot-glue gun (These come in a variety of costs and sizes, but the type with a trigger is preferable.)
- A saw (You can obtain a small, inexpensive coping saw at the hardware or dollar store.)
- An electric engraver (Sometimes called an "electric pencil," also obtained at the hardware store.)
- Scissors, white glue, a hammer, etc. (usually already part of your household equipment).

Safety First

Please use and store all tools safely. The hot-glue gun is one of the most dangerous of all tools if you are not careful when handling it. Obtain a piece of scrap board to use as a pad for your gun. Unplug the glue gun when you aren't using it. If you dribble some of the glue on your fingers, *do not try* to pull it off! Instead, immediately immerse your hand in cold water. Pulling hot glue off will bring skin with it and continue the burn; immersing it stops the burn.

When using the electric engraver, always wear safety glasses to prevent metal or glass chips from flying and hitting your eye.

Herbal Medicine

Although herbal medicines have been used for centuries, even the most dedicated herbalist will warn you that in case of serious illness you should follow the advice of your doctor. Herbal projects in this book are not intended, nor claimed, as any type of medicinal cure. Consult your doctor for health problems.

Ann Ball

The Garden of Eden
and the Beginnings of Gardening

Gardens of the Bible

The scriptural home of our first parents was a garden.

"And the Lord God had planted a paradise of pleasure from the beginning: wherein he placed man whom he had formed. And the Lord God brought forth of the ground all manner of trees, fair to behold, and pleasant to eat of; the tree of life also in the midst of paradise and the tree of knowledge of good and evil" (Genesis 2:8-9). "And the Lord God took man, and put him into the paradise of pleasure, to dress it, and to keep it" (Genesis 2:15).

Where was the Garden of Eden and what plants grew there? Bible scholars and archaeologists have studied this question for centuries and we still have few answers to many questions.

Although tradition has sometimes designated the apple as the forbidden fruit, most scholars and botanists say the soil and climate were not suitable at that time for their growth, although apples flourish in Israel today. The most likely candidate for the fruit Eve ate is the apricot, with the first runner-up being the citron, which resembles a large lemon.

What scholars can agree on is that the root words for "garden," "Eden," and "paradise" all have connotations of beauty and pleasure, and that then, as now, man has related the elements of nature to the Supreme Being.

Early plant knowledge was passed on verbally. As both the body of knowledge and populations grew, information began to be recorded, and many of the earliest writings are about plants that were important in all facets of life. Babylonian clay tablets from 3000 B.C. illustrate medical treatments and record herbal information. Over the next 1,000 years, parallel cultures in China, Assyria, Egypt, and India developed a written record that included many medicinal plants. Early Western records of herbs describe a mixture of medicinal and magical uses of plants, and Egyptian writings dating from

1550 B.C. contain medical prescriptions and notes on the aromatic and cosmetic uses of herbs. The most ancient gardens were herb gardens. Twenty centuries before Christ's birth, herb traders appear in the Bible when Joseph's brothers sell him to a company of Ishmaelites who came from Gilead with their camels, bearing spicery, balm, and myrrh to Egypt.

Our pre-Christian ancestors, lacking today's scientific knowledge, attributed all sorts of magical properties to plants. They did not have to be trained botanists to observe and appreciate the diversity of the plant world. From time immemorial, dependent on plants for material needs, our ancestors naturally turned to them for aid in the struggle to achieve mastery over their environment and fate. Since plants seemed magical, if man could only harness their power it could be used for relief from misfortune and disease, and through that power man could control his future, making peace with his gods. As long as ignorance kept people enslaved to superstition, the idea of magical plants remained powerful and infiltrated every phase of life.

The ancient Egyptians, extremely attentive to the worship of their gods, entwined their daily life with magic and lore from the plant world. The Greeks developed many legends and myths to explain the mystical properties of plants. The Romans studiously began cataloging observations about the natural world. The most outstanding treatise of plant lore that has survived from ancient times is that of the Roman Gaius Plinius Secundus, known to modern readers as Pliny. His massive 37-volume work is a fascinating compilation of fact and fiction. Many plants, especially flowers, were exorcised of their pagan connotations by a new association with Christian saints and martyrs. As the Christian missionaries spread across Europe, they converted flowers as well as people.

It is often said that the monasteries were the pioneers of garden-making in Europe's Middle Ages. It seems that the founders of the monasteries took over from the Roman Italians the idea of schools-in-gardens and the idea of the *villa rustica* supporting the community with its produce. But even Augustine was not altogether an innovator in modeling a Christian establishment on the pagan house-and-garden complex, for the oldest Byzantine basilicas had adjoining porticoes called "paradises" that were planted as gardens. These cloister gardens were the first real gardens of the European Middle Ages and were being planted at least as early as the eighth century. Vegetable gardens associated with monastic foundations are even earlier than these ecclesiastical paradises. This was at least partly due to St.

Benedict, whose sixth-century rule enjoined self-sufficiency in vegetables and herbs on his disciples, and work in the garden for everyone. The Benedictines improved gardening techniques throughout the Middle Ages.

Flowers began to be important for their own sake about the sixth or seventh century, when the Church quit condemning them as heathenish and took over their use in ritual and symbolism.

The advancement of gardening in the eleventh and twelfth centuries in Europe was not solely in ecclesiastical hands. Secular lords soon learned the worth of the garden from the Church, and traveling soldier-noblemen and priests brought ideas from what they had seen in Norman Sicily. The nobles of northern Europe caught the taste for gardens from the churchmen. The ladies became the castle gardeners, and like the monks, they planted vegetables, salad greens, medicinal herbs, and flowers. Contacts between West and East influenced garden design and provided a slow enrichment of plant materials.

By the fourteenth century, interest in gardening began to spread from the nobility to the class of burgesses, in France and in Germany, where some of the great cities were not far behind the Italians. We don't know as much about the smaller gardens. At least in the north they had lawns; they were usually enclosed within walls or clipped evergreen hedges. They had beds of aromatic herbs and some flowers, certainly roses, lilies, and violets. They made much use of evergreens and they also made use of topiary art.

After Charles VII of France invaded Italy in 1495, he returned home with many Italian artists and four tons of artistic loot to begin transforming his country into a paradise. The artists included a gardener, the priest Pasello da Mercogliano, who began the work of bringing the Italian influence to France. Charles's successors shared his passion for beautifying his country, and even today France is known for some of the most beautiful gardens in the world.

In England, gardening remained very backward during the fifteenth century because of social conditions unfavorable to an art which demands peace, plenty, and time. With the accession of Henry VII and the success of his peace-keeping, money-accumulating policy, a change occurred. The great men of the day, such as Cardinal Wolsey and St. Thomas More, had the taste and inclination to patronize artists, including garden artists. By the mid-sixteenth century, because of the great wealth and importance of such cities as Augsburg, Germany had urban gardens before any other country in Europe (except Italy).

The discovery of the New World enriched gardening in both directions. Previously unknown and new species of plants — and many uses for them — began to travel across the ocean, not just across a continent. With the advent of the industrial revolution, even greater exchanges were made. Modern agriculture has developed into a refined science, but small home gardens remain pleasurable for many families.

Throughout the history of gardening, Catholic traditions regarding the subject have developed and intertwined fact and legend with natural history. The following pages will examine some of these traditions and provide modern projects to celebrate the goodness of God's earth.

Make a Blooming Gardening Hat

Supplies needed

wide-brimmed straw hat

silk flowers

hot-glue gun

scarf or bandana (optional)

scarf or ribbon (optional)

Do you have a "black" thumb? Then why not make a gardening hat that makes it appear as if you have a "green" thumb? It is functional, as it keeps the sun from melting you while you are working outside, and makes a pretty accent when hung on a wall by the door leading out to the garden. For that matter, it makes a lovely decoration for the front door to signify to passers-by that a gardener lives at your house.

Read all the directions before beginning this project; the beauty of hot glue is that it makes an immediate bond.

You may, of course, use all-new materials for your hat. You can also recycle and make this hat from pre-used materials. Look for a hat in a garage sale or forgotten closet. We obtained our silk flowers at the crafts store. They had fallen off the wire stems and were packaged for quick sale in a large bag for a very inexpensive price.

Directions

To use silk flowers from a previous arrangement, take the stems out of the foam or clay that is holding them. Swish each stem through a pan of soapy water. Rinse and hang them over the bathtub to dry with the flower heads pointing down. Although some of the artificial flowers don't take well to a bath, most do fine. For flowers that have a few ragged edges, give them a light spray with a clear polyethylene paint. When dry, use nail scissors to trim.

Carefully remove flower heads and leaves from the stems. Plug in your hot-glue gun to warm up. If you have never used a glue gun, be certain to read all the cautions, as this can be one of the most dangerous of tools if not used with extreme care. You may want to practice briefly on some scrap materials to see how quickly and well this type of glue holds.

If your hat is to be worn, use a small bandana or scarf to glue a liner on the inside edge of the crown where the hat touches your head. This step is not necessary if your hat is to be used for decoration only. My friend Carmen's mother used to tell us that ladies didn't sweat — they glowed. Well, I "glow" a lot when I am working in my garden, so the liner keeps the "glow" off my brow and out of my eyes when I am hard at work.

Begin at the center of the back and apply the glue to the hat in a 2"-wide squiggle, a few inches at a time. Press the scarf into the hot glue carefully. The scarf does not have to be perfectly flat but should rather be slightly gathered to make a more effective "glow-catcher." Tuck the ends of the scarf under and hold with a dab of glue at the point where they join. If you like, add a single flower or a small bunch at this joining.

Next, turn your hat over and glue on a thin scarf or a wide ribbon to make a band. Allow the ends to dangle over the back of the hat if you like. Apply the band just as you did the inner band by putting squiggles of glue on the hat and pressing the fabric into the glue.

Blooming Gardening Hat

Glue on some leaves for greenery. Place the leaves with their branch end toward the band of the hat; have some leaves pointing up toward the crown and some pointing out toward the brim. When working with flowers, always use an odd number; this rule applies to the leaves as well. Now, as with the flowers, you will be placing the glue on the leaves, not the hat. Small amounts will suffice to hold the leaves firm. Apply the glue to the leaf and then press the leaf with firmness onto the hat.

Arrange the flower heads you intend to use in a line on the table, to see the effect. Pick flowers whose colors look good together; discard those that make a jarring note. We used flowers that shaded from pink to purple with white accents, but a mixture of colors can also be attractive. Choose either the front or the back of the crown as your focal point, where you will use your largest flowers.

To glue on your flowers, pinch the petals together and apply glue generously to the plastic part at the bottom of each blossom. Press the flower firmly in place, holding it tightly against the hat for about 10 seconds. When the glue has begun to harden, release the petals and fluff them into shape with your fingers. Begin by placing your largest flowers at the focal point and medium flowers around the crown. Use the smaller flowers to go back and fill in any gaps.

If your hat is to be used as a decoration or accent piece only, you can make a wire loop from an unbent paperclip to use as a hanger.

The Hanging Gardens of Babylon

Over 2,500 years ago, King Nebuchadnezzar II of Babylon created a beautiful set of terraced gardens in the arid region of the country now known as Iraq. One of the earliest "travel writers," Philon of Byzantium, listed the gardens as one of the "seven wonders of the world." (A number of early writers made lists of the outstanding things created by man which they saw on their travels. Most of these lists of "wonders" numbered seven, probably because the number seven had a magical significance for many early peoples.) Later, the fifth-century Greek historian, Herodotus, wrote a full description of the gardens in all their glory.

Babylonia lay in the flat land of Mesopotamia and had no mountains. Nebuchadnezzar's young bride came from the mountainous region of Persia. Possibly as a gift to delight her with reminders of her homeland, the King had his workmen raise an artificial mountain about 350 feet high. This was built on the banks of the Euphrates River, which flowed through the royal city. Terraced with a series of platforms, the mountain was planted with trees, lawns, and flowers. Water from the Euphrates and from wells in the foundation of the mountain's construction was pumped to the top of the hill and flowed down through artificial brooks and miniature waterfalls. The water was also used to irrigate the plants. In the hot, arid land, the gardens, which seemed to hang in the air, became a haven of coolness and beauty.

Excavations in our own century brought to light what is left of the gardens of Babylon from under 2,000 years of rubble. The German archaeologist Robert Koldewey (1855-1925) traced the foundations of what is believed to have been the famous Hanging Gardens.

The wondrous Hanging Gardens of Babylon inspired the design for two simple projects to make from PVC pipe: a hanging herb garden for the kitchen and the lovely hanging garden accents for your flowerbed.

Babylonian Hanging Herb Garden

First, use nail polish remover to erase as much as possible of the stamped markings on the PVC.

Using PVC cement, glue the shorter pipes along the longer, center pipe, graduating from the tallest to the shortest. PVC cement is extremely flammable and should be used outside or in an open garage, where there is no chance that the fumes can build up. Be certain to read all of the cautions on the container. Place a thin layer of glue along the center pipe and a full layer of glue on the pipe you are gluing. You will need to hold your pipes in place while the cement hardens. Some large rubber bands may be helpful to secure the pipe while the cement dries. You can daub an extra layer of cement between the pipes for more strength.

After several hours, you can add the bottoms to your planter, but wait at least overnight before planting. To fill the bottoms, cut a thick piece of plastic scrub pad in a circle to fit the bottom of each pipe, or scrunch up one of the "scrubbies" until you can poke it into the pipe.

Brush a thick layer of cement in a band about 2" wide inside the bottom of your pipe and push in the pad. Daub on some extra cement and allow it to dry. If the pad does not touch completely on all

Supplies needed

Plastic PVC pipe in the following diameters and lengths. (Some hardware stores will cut the pipe for you, or you can cut the pipe easily with a small hacksaw. You may ask a plumber or construction foreman for scraps and make your planter a different length from ours.)

1 piece ½" diameter and 24" long

1 piece 2" diameter and 15" long

1 piece 2" diameter and 12" long

1 piece 1½" diameter and 9" long

1 piece 1½"diameter and 6" long

nail-polish remover

small can of PVC cement

4 round, plastic "scrubbie" pads or flat, woven, plastic scrub pads

box of charcoal used in fish-tank filters (or broken pieces of barbecue charcoal)

½" washer

medium "s" hook

plastic clothesline

sand

potting soil

small herb plants

Hanging Herb Garden

sides, you can fill in with small pieces, attaching each with the cement.

When the cement in your construction is completely dry, make a hanger using plastic clothesline cord, an "s" hook, and a washer. Cut a piece of cord about 54" long. Tie a knot around the bottom of the "s" hook midway on the cord, leaving two equal ends. Thread the ends through your center piece of PVC pipe and through a washer on the bottom. Pull the cord taut so that the "s" hook is directly at the top of the pipe. Tie a square knot large enough not to slip through the washer. Instead of cutting off the excess ends, you can attach them to the underside of the planter with PVC cement for extra strength if you like.

When you are ready to plant, add a layer of charcoal an inch or two high in each pipe first. You can use the type from the pet store or smash up some charcoal briquettes with a hammer. The charcoal will help to keep your dirt smelling sweet. An inch or more of sand added to each pipe next will help provide the good drainage that most herbs prefer. Then add potting soil.

Plant a different herb in each pipe. Some good choices are oregano, rosemary, thyme, or mint. The smaller herbs will work best. You can grow garlic for its foliage, but it will eventually outgrow the planter, and of course you cannot harvest the bulb when you grow it this way. Ask your garden shop for suggestions and try to plant herbs that you often use for cooking; you can trim your plants and use the trimmings whenever you need to flavor a favorite dish.

Hang your herb garden in a sunny window inside or on your porch or patio. Most herbs appreciate being misted with water from a spray bottle. If you hang them over the kitchen sink, you won't have to mist so often. Do not over-water! Most herb plants like water, but prefer to keep their "feet" (roots) dry. Since the bottom of your planter will allow water to run through freely, take the planter to the sink when you water and allow the excess to drain before re-hanging your planter, if you plan to keep it inside the house.

Hanging Garden Accent Wall

Beautiful "hanging" garden accent walls can be made using plastic PVC pipe. We used ours as a backdrop for a small cement statue of Our Lady. You can put several of these accent walls in your garden, or group your pipes in a circular pattern. We used ours for a small accent, but you can adapt much larger pipe for your garden if you like, fitting a clay pot into the top of the pipe instead of actually growing the plants in the pipe.

Directions

Arrange your pipes in the pattern you want. We put the ½" pipe in the center and staggered the other pieces downward.

Dampen the ground. If the ground is very hard, you may have to dig it up first to make it soft enough to drive in your pipe. With the hammer, drive the PVC into the ground at least 3".

To make your pipes less likely to tip or fall over, you can drive a piece of rebar into the ground in the center of each pipe, leaving enough sticking up inside the pipe to help brace the pipe. Of course, you would drive the rebar in before the pipes were driven into the ground, but you should place the pipes to see where the center will be in order to put your rebar in the correct spot.

Supplies needed

1½" PVC cut into lengths of 18", 12", and 6"

2" PVC cut into lengths of 18", 12", and 6"

½" piece of PVC, 24" long

hammer

8" to 10" ceramic or concrete statue

sand

soil

trailing plants

scrap rebar, optional

decorative rock

Pack the soil well around your pipe. Then fill the pipes nearly to the top with sand. The last three to five inches of pipe should be filled with potting soil. Add your plants, choosing those that are appropriate for your climate and the amount of sunshine in the area where you construct your wall. Use decorative white or colored rocks to set off your statue and the front of the wall. You may want to push a piece of wire into the ground and into a hole in the bottom of the statue to help anchor it.

King Solomon, Master Gardener

The Bible describes King Solomon as a master gardener on a huge scale. In Ecclesiastes we read: "I planted me vineyards: I made me gardens and orchards, and I planted trees in them of all kinds of fruits; I made me pools of water, to water therewith the wood that bringeth forth trees" (Ecclesiastes 2:4-6). Archaeologists have not located the exact place of Solomon's gardens, but we can suppose they were close to his palace. A few miles outside of Jerusalem are three large reservoirs that have traditionally been called the Pools of Solomon, and these may be ones he constructed to provide the water for his gardens. We will never know the exact layout of the gardens or the names of all the plants he grew in them. However, we can construct a general picture of these gardens based on Scripture and on archaeological knowledge of other gardens in the Holy Land at that time. What was referred to as a "garden" was actually several gardens close together. Each one was probably rectangular in shape and walled. The sides of the walls were usually masked by hedges.

There would be a garden for olive trees and another for nut trees. Walnuts, pistachios, and almonds would be favorites for this garden. The almond, one of the most valued trees of the ancient world, was associated with rebirth of life, since it is the first of all trees in the Holy Land to flower, producing its blossoms sometimes as early as January while its branches are still bare of leaves.

The most unusual of the gardens must have been devoted to spices. Solomon's trade with foreign lands, such as Arabia and India, brought many exotic plants. From India came the eaglewood tree, which exuded a fragrant gum called "aloes" in the Old Testament. (The New Testament aloes come from a different plant.) Also from India came the calamus, whose stem and leaves smelled strongly of ginger. From the Himalaya Mountains of Asia traders brought the spice called spikenard. The hairy stem of this small plant gives off a rich fragrance. Spikenard was extremely expensive, and its dried stems became an important trade item in the ancient world. Mary of Bethany anointed the feet of Jesus with ointment from this.

In addition to the glitter of his court, his exotic gardens, and animals, Solomon's wisdom about wild things was famous throughout the ancient world. One proverb of his, often quoted, is:

"Go to the ants, thou sluggard; consider her ways and be wise: Which having no guide, overseer, or ruler, provideth her meat in the summer, and gathereth her food in the harvest" (Proverbs 6:6-8).

Just as Solomon praised the lowly ant, recognizing the wisdom of even this smallest of beasts, as gardeners we should attempt to understand and appreciate the value of the wildlife in our gardens.

Butterflies, bees, bats, birds, and other small critters populate gardens in country and city, although some are rarely seen. Some, like the butterfly, are welcome, both for their beauty and for their assistance in pollinating many plants. Some, such as snakes, rats, and rabbits, are often unwelcome guests. Still others, the lowly bat a case in question, are simply misunderstood.

Make a Toad Abode

Toads eat many insects, and are common denizens of many gardens. In one summer, a toad can eat about 10,000 insects. It also eats beetles, spiders, and snails. Children can make a home for one of these helpful little critters as well as an attractive accent for a shady spot in your garden, using an old clay flowerpot, acrylic paints, and imagination.

Supplies needed

medium-size clay flowerpot

acrylic paints

paintbrush

Directions

Wash and dry the flowerpot if it has dirt on it.

Paint on any design you think a toad would like. For brighter colors, paint the design in white first and then go over it with the colors. Let the paint dry.

Find a good, shady hiding place outside. Turn the dirt to a depth of about an inch in an area a little wider than your toad abode. Bury the pot on its side with about ⅓ of the pot in the dirt. Put a little dirt inside, making certain it is damp and crumbly. You can put a few dead leaves inside, too.

You will know when your toad abode acquires a tenant because the dirt at the front of the house will get worn down from the toad sitting there waiting for his dinner to pass by.

Make a Butterfly House

In order to survive in the winter, a number of species of American butterflies either migrate or hibernate. Those who over-winter choose dark, sheltered places for protection from the cold. These species often hibernate from late August to April or May. During the winter, butterflies may choose to over-winter in a butterfly box; during the summer, they may use it as protection from predators.

You can build a butterfly house from our

Toad Abode

basic directions. Let your imagination take over and make your own design, or follow our directions to copy ours. After your box is ready, put some pine bark mulch or tree bark loosely inside it. In warm weather, place your box at a height of three to four feet near flowering plants. You can mount it on a pole, a post, or a fence. During cold months, put your butterfly box in a sheltered spot, protected from the wind.

You can cut your own boards, or work from a kit. Kits for butterfly houses are available at many arts and crafts stores.

Directions

In one of your 4"x11"x½" boards, cut 4 entry slits. Each slit is ½" wide by 3¼" long. The easiest way to begin these slits is to mark a spot 1¼" from the top and 1¼" from the side at each corner of your board. Drill a hole at each of these marks.

Next, measure 3¼" from each hole toward the

Supplies needed

18- 1½" finishing nails
2- 1½" screws (optional)
2 screws
2- 4"x11"x½" boards
2- 5¼"x11"x½" boards
1- 6"x6"x½" board
1- 4"x3 ¾"x½" board
drill with ½" bit
small coping saw or jig saw
white paint for outdoor use
acrylic paints
small brush
bottle of gold fabric-paint

center of the board. Drill 4 more holes. Slip your saw into each hole about halfway around the circle and cut down to the other hole. Repeat on the other side of the circle. In this way, you can form 4 oval entry slits wide enough for a butterfly and too narrow for its predators to enter.

Lightly sand all outer faces of your boards.

Lay the 2, 4"x11" boards (the front and back of your butterfly box) on their long ½" edges, making certain their outer sides are facing out. Carefully align one of the 5¼"x11" boards on top, making edges flush. Tack in place with one nail on each side, but do not drive the nail completely home until you have centered the other side. Turn the box over and repeat with the other 5¼"x11" board. When all edges are flush, use nails at both ends to secure the sides.

Fit the 4"x3¾" board into the end of the assembled box to make the floor. If the floor does not easily slide into position, sand the edges until it fits. Secure the floor with nails, or screws. If you use screws, you can later take the flooring out to clean the box after a couple of years' use.

Fill the box about half-full of pine-bark mulch or bark pieces. Then nail on the roof board, letting the top stick out over the front and making the back of the roof flush with the back of the box.

Paint your butterfly box white. Spray enamel or any exterior grade white paint will do. When paint is dry, paint flowers on all sides of box to attract the butterflies.

Butterfly House

To make the vining black-eyed Susans shown in our illustration, begin by painting the vines and leaves. Starting at the bottom, brush green paint up in a slightly curved line, 3" or 4" long. At the point of the curve, make another curved line with the curve flowing in the opposite direction. Continue making curves until you have nearly reached the top. Repeat this process for a second vine.

At the end of each curve, paint a heart-shaped leaf. Next paint 5 or 7 brown circles about ½" in diameter near the vines. One or 2 can actually be painted on the vines, but most should be off the vine in open white areas. Art teachers always say to use an odd number when making floral compositions; we don't know why, but it does look better. Allow the vines and centers to dry in order to avoid runs.

Load a small (#2) pointed brush with deep yellow paint. Place the pointed tip on the edge of one of the circular centers and "sit down" the brush to make a teardrop-shaped petal. Repeat from a point exactly opposite the first petal. Make a third petal from a point on the circle halfway between the 2 previous petals; a fourth opposite the third. Then put a petal between each of the petals you have already painted. Make 8 dark-yellow petals on each flower. Switch to light-yellow paint and make shorter petals in between the darker ones, overlapping until petals completely rim each flower.

When you have completed painting your flowers, allow the project to dry completely. Spray your butterfly house with several coats of clear acrylic paint to help weatherproof it.

If you like, you can highlight the centers of your flowers with gold fabric paint.

Supplies needed

acrylic paints

piece of balsa wood, ¾"x¾"x1"

2 pieces of balsa, 1"x1¼"x⅛"

tiny twig

glue

pencil

small eye hook

10" to 12" of green florist wire

craft knife or coping saw

Make a Bug House

You can make a bug house to brighten up your potted plants. Since most people would rather the bugs stayed outside, however, ours is just for looks and not an invitation to occupancy. These are simple to make and a group of them would make clever ornaments for a Christmas "nature" tree.

Directions

Balsa wood is sold in strips of ⅛" thick wood and square rods at most model shops. The wood is very soft and easily cut with a craft knife or the small coping saw. You could use a small block of any type of soft wood for the house; we suggest balsa for its ease in handling.

With the lead end of a pencil, punch a small

hole about ⅛" deep, in the center of the cut end of your block. Punch another hole underneath the first one about halfway between the center hole and the point of the block. See diagram. Twirl the pencil to make the second hole a tiny bit larger and deeper than the first.

Paint the block white. When dry, paint the center hole black to simulate the entrance.

Break off a tiny piece of your twig about ⅜" long. Paint it brown. You could also use a piece from the center of a toothpick if you can't find a twig small enough. Glue the twig into the bottom hole.

Paint both pieces of your roof red on both sides, being careful to paint the edges as well. When they are thoroughly dry, glue them on to form the roof, letting the long end lap over the front side of the house.

Bug House assembly

Center the eye hook at the top of the roof. Twist a stiff piece of wire through the eye hook and bend a curve so the house will dangle down and the rest of the wire can stick in a potted plant.

If you are making the houses as tree ornaments you can use a Christmas tree hanger instead of the long wire. Joanna made a dozen of these years ago; one still graces a potted plant and the others hang on our Christmas tree each year.

Last year, Virginia Murthough brought Karin a mosquito house. Similar in construction, Karin's house was carved into the shape of Noah's Ark. Instead of being hung on a wire, this house was glued to a

Bug House

thin wood dowel. Karin told me the theory of the mosquito house is to put them in plants with the hope that all the mosquitoes will stay at home!

The Agony in the Garden of Gethsemane

After eating a last supper with his disciples, Our Lord, according to his custom, went to the Mount of Olives with them to pray. Beyond the Cedron (also called Kidron) Valley, there was a garden into which he and his disciples entered. He walked a little ways from them and, kneeling, began to pray by saying, "Father, if thou art willing, remove this cup from me; yet not my will but thine be done." An angel came to strengthen him and, falling into an agony, his sweat became as drops of blood. When he finished his prayer, he returned to the disciples, finding them asleep. He woke them and told them to pray that they would not fall into temptation.

Refer to

Matthew 26:36-56

Mark 14: 26-49

Luke 22:39-53

John 18:1-12

At that time, a crowd came out, led by Judas Iscariot. The scene was illuminated by lanterns and torches, and the Roman soldiers were carrying weapons. When his disciples saw what was coming, one of them struck one of the Roman soldiers with a sword and cut off his ear. Cautioning his disciples to bear with them, Jesus touched the man's ear and healed it. He asked the chief priests and captains of the temple and elders who had come for him why they came, as if he were a criminal. Then, telling them, "But this is your hour and the power of darkness," he allowed himself to be led away to the high priest's house.

Christ's agony in the Garden of Gethsemane has caught the imagination of artists, writers, and poets through the centuries. The scene is shown in numerous paintings. Correggio, Paul Veronese, Abrecht Dürer, and Rembrandt have all painted powerful pictures of this subject. Poems and prose works also memorialize this event, and the overtones of gloom and sadness generally overlay all the depictions. One poem which I recall vividly from my childhood portrays the pathos of the struggle of Jesus during the dark hours before his arrest, but also includes the beauty of nature, the Master's reverent devotion to the will of His Heavenly Father, and associates the life and death of Christ with the trees in whose shade He often rested and which he sought out as a place of quiet meditation and prayer.

The poem, "A Ballad of Trees and the Master," was written by Sydney

Lanier (1842-1881). A native of Georgia, Lanier served as a soldier in the Confederate Army, and later practiced law and taught school before his early death at the age of 39. A great religious poem becomes a hymn when it is set to music, and in 1904, Lanier's poem was set to a beautiful, haunting melody by Peter C. Lutkin and became used in many churches.

> Into the woods my Master went,
> Clean for-spent, for-spent;
> Into the woods my Master came,
> For-spent with love and shame.
> But the olives they were not blind to Him,
> The little gray leaves were kind to Him,
> The thorn-tree had a mind to Him,
> When into the woods He came.
>
> Out of the woods my Master went,
> And He was well content;
> Out of the woods my Master came,
> Content with death and shame.
> When death and shame would woo Him last,
> From under the trees they drew Him last,
> 'Twas on a tree they slew Him last,
> When out of the woods He came.

What type of garden was this, where Jesus spent his final night of freedom after the Last Supper? The garden of Gethsemane lay on the slopes of the Mount of Olives. Not a flower garden, its name means "olive presses," and it was where the olive trees grew and olive oil was pressed. At the time of Christ, the Mount of Olives was covered with a luxuriant growth of olive trees and people often came from Jerusalem to seek relief from the blazing sun. About forty years after Christ spent the night on the Mount, the Romans cut down the grove, but the trees sprung again from the same roots. Cutting down an olive tree actually rejuvenates it, and new vigorous sprouts are sent up from the roots. These roots are extremely long-lived and it is almost impossible to kill an olive tree just by chopping it down.

After the flood, Noah sent a dove to seek land. On the second attempt, the dove returned with the leaf of an olive in its bill. This was evidence that the waters had subsided enough to expose the valleys where olive trees grew, promising a rebirth of life. The olive tree was the symbol of peace in the ancient world, so it was fitting that it was associated with Jesus, who was also known as the Prince of Peace. Pressed and dried leaves from an olive tree are among the common souvenirs taken by many of the visitors to the Holy Land, as are little cards with pressed flowers.

The olive was the most important tree cultivated in the area, and it is still the most characteristic tree in the landscape. Many-branched and growing more than twenty feet high, with a gnarled trunk and evergreen leaves, it is native only to the lands bordering the Mediterranean Sea, and is well-adapted to conditions there. It can endure long periods of drought and can grow in poor soil. In biblical times, a single, large olive tree could provide an entire

family with the oil it needed for food and lamps. As much as half a ton of oil could be pressed in a year. Because both the unripened and the ripe fruit of the tree is edible, the crop is year-round. The ancient farmer could gather his olive crop whenever his work in the fields allowed time. When ripe, the fruit turned black, and was harvested by beating the branches with long poles, knocking the olives off. Not all of the fruit was shaken from the tree, however, because it was customary to leave some on the boughs for the poor, orphans, and widows to gather.

Flower Press with decorated cover

All the evangelists directed attention to the garden of Gethsemane. Early Christians soon made it a place of prayer and pilgrimage. Pilgrimages are described as early as A.D. 333 by the Pilgrim of Bordeaux, who visited there, and by Petronius, the bishop of Bologna, c. 420. St. Jerome, in translating the *Onomasticon* of Eusebius, adds to the article that a church is "now" built there. St. Sylvia of Aquitania, c. 385-388, relates that on Holy Thursday the procession coming down from the Mount of Olives made a station at the beautiful church built on the spot where Jesus underwent the agony, and then descended to Gethsemane, where Christ was taken prisoner. The church was destroyed by the Persians in 614, rebuilt by the Crusaders, and finally razed in the early part of the

1200s. Described by a number of early writers from the seventh through the twelfth centuries, the foundations of this Church of the Agony were uncovered by archaeologists in our own time. A fragmentary account of a pilgrimage in the fourth century mentions "a grotto at the place where the Jews took the Saviour captive." Tradition assigns this grotto as a place where Christ often took refuge with His disciples in the evening hours. Theodosius (c. 530) described the grotto as the place where the Lord supped with His disciples, and where he washed their feet. "There are to be seen four benches where Our Lord reclined in the midst of His Apostles. Each bench can seat three persons. There also, Judas betrayed the Savior. Some persons, when they visit this spot, through devotion partake of some refreshment, but no meat. They light torches because the place is in a grotto." Ancient writings place the Garden of Gethsemane about 130 feet from this grotto. The garden itself is quadrangular in shape, about 195 feet on each side. Olive trees extant in our time are considered to be offshoots of those from the time of Christ.

Make a Flower Press

You can make a simple flower press to help you preserve and use small and beautiful flowers and leaves. Even city dwellers can locate many flowers worth pressing on a short walk almost anywhere where something is growing. Don't overlook the weeds! One gardener once pointed out that "a weed is only a flower whose virtues have not yet been discovered." Think "small," and among the tiniest specimens of nature you may discover a large amount of beauty.

Supplies needed

2 rectangles of ¼" plywood, 11"x9"

scraps of cardboard

4 bolts, 3½" long

4 washers and 4 wing-nuts to fit bolts

heavy white paper; acid-free is best

drill

acrylic paints (optional)

Directions

Clamp or hold your plywood rectangles together, then drill holes in each of the 4 corners to fit your bolts. Ours were drilled about an inch in from the edge of the board.

Cut about half-a-dozen rectangles from cardboard, a little smaller than your boards so they can fit inside, then clip the corners to allow the cardboard to fit inside the bolt holes.

Use one of your pieces of cardboard as a pattern and cut heavy white paper to sandwich between each of your cardboard pieces.

Paint or stencil a design on your covers if you like, using acrylic paints. In addition to its function, a decorated flower-press makes an interesting conversation piece.

Thread bolts through the bottom cover. Layer 4 pieces of cardboard and white paper and slip on the top cover, securing bolts with the washers and wing nuts. (You should have: cover, cardboard, 2 pieces of white papers, another piece of cardboard, and the bottom board of the flower press.)

After a collecting expedition, lay your specimens between the pieces of white paper, arranging them carefully using tweezers and a toothpick when necessary. Tighten the covers to hold and press your tiny flowers and leaves until they are dry, about a week minimum.

Some Tips on Pressing and Using Flowers

In the process of pressing your flowers, you will probably ruin some of them, so gather more than you need. Don't forget to look for small, interesting leaves as well. Larger flowers don't press well, so hunt for the tiniest of blooms. Even most forms of grass have flowers.

Many herbs not only dry well but add a lovely odor to your projects.

Some flowers will not hold their color well; trial and error will show you the ones that make the prettiest projects. Some flowers "bleed" while drying, so don't place flowers too close to each other on your pages.

Putting the flower press together

A pair of tweezers and a toothpick are indispensable tools when working with the dried specimens, as well as when arranging them for pressing.

The tiniest dots of white craft-glue are all that is necessary; toothpicks make a good tool for applying the glue.

You can use dried flowers to make bookmarks; laminate these with clear contact or laminating paper. Pressed flowers can decorate the front of inexpensive stationery or cards, to grace a note to a friend. Pictures incorporating this type of flower have been popular off and on for many years. Framed behind glass, the flowers hold their beauty for many years. A thoughtful gift for a friend can be made by adding pressed flowers to a sentiment written in calligraphy, or a small religious picture, and framing it in an inexpensive but attractive frame. You can ornament a simple wooden frame by gluing on dried flowers and, when dry, spraying the frame with multiple coats of clear spray, allowing each to dry before adding the next.

Frame a Picture With Flowers

You can use your dried flowers to decorate a picture of Our Lord, Our Lady, or one of the saints. The picture makes a graceful accent for your home and a tribute to the saint portrayed. I chose a modern icon of Our Lady of Guadalupe, Mother of the Americas, that I cut from the cover of a magazine. The icon is an unusual representation of the Guadalupe image because it shows her holding the child Jesus. We picked Guadalupe because of its association with the roses that Our Lady left in the *tilma* (cloak) of Blessed Juan Diego. Any colored print that you like is fine; you can look for one from a magazine or obtain a print from your local religious-goods store. My friend LaNell decorated and framed a Christmas card depicting St. Joseph the Worker. She did not need to back her print with colored paper. Her arrangement of deep-colored field-flowers and spikey leaves gives depth to the monochrome tones in the print.

Directions

Cut a sheet of colored paper to fit your frame area. Choose a color that will go well with your print and with the colors of the flowers you have

> **Supplies needed**
>
> colored print of Our Lord, Our Lady, or one of the saints
>
> a frame with glass larger than your picture
>
> colored paper sized to fit the frame, for a background to the picture
>
> pressed flowers and leaves
>
> glue stick
>
> white craft-glue
>
> small paintbrush
>
> tweezers
>
> a toothpick
>
> small container to mix your glue

dried. We used a pale-blue parchment to pick up the tones in Our Lady's mantle. Do not use construction paper that children use in school; this type of

Picture framed with flowers

paper fades rapidly. Typing or copy paper, stationary, or even a brown paper-sack will hold their colors much better.

Paste your print to the middle of your paper; use a glue stick or other paper paste. Leave a border at least an inch wide between your print and the frame to allow room for your flowers. You can leave your print in its rectangle shape, or trim around the image.

Carefully, using tweezers and a toothpick as tools to help you move the delicate flowers, lay out your design on the print. You can border the entire print with flowers or decorate only the bottom and one side of the print. We made a crown for Our Lady, and placed a tiny dried rose in her left hand.

In a small container, dilute white craft-glue with half as much water. Using this mixture, glue the leaves first, then the flowers.

Holding your pressed specimens with your tweezers, use your paintbrush to carefully brush a small amount of glue on the back of your leaf or flower. Dried flowers are very delicate and the addition of the glue must be done with great care. Hopefully you will have dried more specimens than you need because a number of them will undoubtedly break as you are working with them.

Continue gluing until you have completed your pattern. Allow your print to dry for several hours before framing so that excess glue will not seep up and mar the glass. Wou can hang your floral tribute or set it on your family altar when framed.

Floral Notes

You can use some of your most delicate pressed-flowers to create one-of-a-kind note cards for special messages to special friends. Make them for yourself and for gifts.

We used Strathmore-brand blank greeting cards, which we obtained at an artists' supply store, but you can cut heavy paper to fit standard envelopes.

Supplies needed

plain note cards with envelopes to fit

dried flowers and leaves

white craft-glue

crystal-clear glitter

tweezers

scissors

watercolors and small brush

Directions

First, using a small brush and green watercolor paint diluted with plenty of water, make some feathery strokes from the bottom left side of the card's front toward the top of the card. These will simulate stems for your dried flowers and leaves. The stem should have a center stroke that goes about halfway straight up the height of the card and several side strokes that curve slightly toward the edge of the card.

We used blue deckle-edge cards that had a blue stripe across the bottom of the front of the card. If you are making your own cards, you may want to paint a line across the bottom of the front of the card.

Allow your watercolors to dry thoroughly.

In a small container, mix white glue half-and-half with water.

Floral notes

Use your tweezers to help you arrange a pretty pattern of dried flowers and leaves over your stems. When you are satisfied with your arrangement, paint the glue onto the card where the flower or leaf is to go and lay the dried specimen on the glue.

Using more glue mixture, paint over the top of the flowers and leaves, making certain each is flat against the card. Don't use dried flowers with too much bulk; the flatter the flower, the better.

Before the glue dries, take a small pinch of clear glitter and dust it lightly over the design.

Allow cards to dry thoroughly. If any of the flowers seem to be sticking up from the card, you can add a dab of the glue mixture and re-stick them. When the cards are thoroughly dry, store them in a box or tie several of the cards and envelopes with a pretty ribbon to present them as a gift to a friend.

Bible and Medieval Gardens

Since about the turn of the century, many people have planted Bible gardens. These are gardens in which the plants are selected according to those referenced in Scripture.

As we have pointed out, the most ancient gardens were herb gardens where the plants were valued for their uses in medicines, cookery, and fragrance, as well as for their beauty. Early trade caravans sprang up to exchange the wealth of these plants. Twenty centuries before the birth of Christ, as Genesis 37:25 tells us, young Joseph's brothers sold him into slavery to traders in spices, balm, and myrrh.

In the New Testament, Jesus' parables were stories for simple people who lived close to the land and the sea. A master storyteller, He drew parallels with the things around the people — things they understood, including many references to local flower and plant life.

Today, many people and organizations grow Bible gardens as a window on history. Many references and stories of the Bible seem more clear when we can see, smell, and touch the plants referred to.

Some examples: To the new settlers in Israel in 1948, it seemed hopeless to make the barren land fruitful again. However, all over the country, Israeli scientists are working to build back growth, often using the Bible for clues to how the ancient residents of the land gardened and farmed. At Boys Town in Nebraska, one of the gardens contains over 150 plants that recall biblical times. Pat Cowan, a professional flower arranger from San Antonio, Texas, turned a passing interest in the flora of the Bible into a lifelong learning adventure, giving talks and demonstrations on biblical-flower themes. Keep your eyes open — articles are often printed in contemporary magazines celebrating Bible gardening adventures.

One of the most interesting and extensive Bible gardens in the United States is the Rodef Shalom Biblical Botanical Garden in Pittsburgh, Pennsylvania. Established on a third of an acre adjacent to the Rodef Shalom Temple, the garden was outlined in the shape of the Land of Israel, and planned to include an area for educational possibilities. After extensive research into the plants of the Bible, construction began in 1986. An international search brought plant specimens from many parts of the world and by the time the garden opened in 1987, its builders had obtained 95 of the 110 species of biblical plants. The gardens contain three ponds, a stream, a beautifully designed waterfall, two bridges, and a pavilion, as well as buildings and walks. They are divided into areas for plants that need varying climates, from desert to semi-tropical. Over 50 species of plants are included, with biblical common names that have provided a ready association with Scripture through the centuries.

The gardens open during the summer from June through mid-September, and lectures and special exhibits highlight an annual theme. Although the garden is open to the public only three months of the year, it is a year-round venture that takes thousands of volunteer hours to prepare for the special exhibits and to maintain the plants and facilities. An avowed purpose of the garden is to bring color and life to the monochromatic black-and-white print of the Bible which, for many people, remains a drab and closed book, according to the garden's founders, Dr. Walter Jacob, senior Rabbi of Temple Rodef Shalom, and Irene Jacob, the director of the garden. Thousands of visitors enjoy the gardens each summer. Thus, the gardens have become a focal point for both Jews and Christians to celebrate an ecumenical high note in the song of their common heritage.

Further information about the Rodef Shalom Biblical Botanical Garden programs may be obtained by writing the director at 4906 Fifth Avenue, Pittsburgh, PA, 15213.

A section of your home garden may be set aside as a biblical garden. Begin by researching the biblical plants and herbs that best fit your area's climate. We list only a few here; a trip to the gardening section of your public library as well as a study of Scripture will give you more ideas. If space allows, you may wish to enhance this area of the garden with a bench or other seating and some sort of water accent to provide a restful place to sit and read your Bible.

Some Biblical Plants

There are many plants named in the Bible, and hundreds of others were favorites of cooks in biblical times. Only a few of the herbs are listed below.

You may want to look up and read, or re-read, the stories in the Bible where they are referenced. Most of these can be easily grown in the United States. Perhaps our list will strike a spark in your imagination for a special focal point or idea to use in making your own Bible garden.

Anise is mentioned in Jesus' rebuke of the Pharisees (Matthew 23:23), although many scholars believe that the word should have been translated as dill, rather than anise. Anise, at any rate, was a favorite of many in biblical times for its strong licorice flavor. In addition to its use in cooking, Kings perfumed their linen with the herb. Later, during the plagues of the Middle Ages, anise was used as a disinfectant. It has also been used as a remedy for indigestion and to sweeten the breath. Recently scientists have discovered that its distinctive odor is a good additive to perfume, as it holds an attraction for many men. A few years ago when traveling on the West Coast above San Francisco, I was startled to see wild anise growing abundantly along the highway.

Bay — In Psalm 37, David mentions the bay tree. In American gardens, the bay laurel with its glossy evergreen leaves is more of a shrub than a tree. In the time of the Greeks and Romans, it was called laurel and its leaves were awarded to the victors in the Olympic Games and to heroes returning from war. The bay laurel can be grown in a pot for many years. Wreaths made of the leaves sweeten and freshen the air in your home, and the leaves are used in many popular recipes.

Coriander — When the children of Israel were wandering in the wilderness, God fed them manna, which "was like coriander seed" (Exodus 16:31). Only the seeds of this annual are called coriander; the leaves of the plant are known as cilantro and are much used in Mexican and some Oriental cuisines.

Cumin — In Isaiah, cumin is one of the herbs mentioned in the lesson of the ploughman (28:25). In the New Testament, Jesus mentions it as one of the herbs the scribes and Pharisees paid tithes on, along with mint and anise (Matthew 23:23). The spicy seed of this annual is used in curry powder and for flavoring chili and stew.

Dill, also mentioned in Matthew, is an easy herb to grow and a favorite with good cooks everywhere. City dwellers can grow this herb in large clay pots on the patio.

Flax — In Proverbs 31:13, the valiant woman who provides for her family has sought wool and flax and made them into cloth by her own handwork. The bright blue flowers and blue-green leaves of flax add a colorful note to the herb garden.

Garlic—While they were wandering in the desert, the Israelites recalled the savor of some of their favorite foods, including meat, cucumbers, melons, leeks, onions, and garlic (Numbers 11:5). Today, there are many varieties of garlic and it is a favorite of cooks in almost every nation. This slow-growing perennial is easy to grow. Separate the bulb into cloves and plant pointed end up, just deep enough in the soil to cover the tops. Apartment dwellers can grow garlic in a pot. When the flavor of garlic is wanted, simply cut and chop one of the leaves, adding it to your recipe for a delicate flavor. When grown outside, the entire plant is dug up to harvest the bulbs.

Hyssop—According to Jewish ritual law, things defiled were purified by sprinkling water from a bunch of hyssop (Psalms 51:9). The hyssop of Bible times was *Origanum syriacum*; the hyssop used in today's gardens belongs to the mint family. It is used in cooking and in making cologne. The attractive evergreen plant is often used as a border.

Mint — There are many varieties of mint, several common in Palestine. Many botanists agree that the mint referred to in the New Testament (Matthew 23:23, Luke 11:42) is horsemint.

Most of the mints grow readily in American gardens, but because of their underground runners tend to take over. It is best to make some sort of barrier if you don't want this to happen. You can knock the bottom off an old pot and sink it into the soil to the rim to contain the mint. Mint can also be grown in a pot on a patio; trimming the top of the plant causes it to bush out. Mint makes a flavorful tea on its own, is a wonderful additive to other teas, and can be used as a flavoring for many sweets. Dried, the leaves and stems make a good addition to potpourri.

Mustard—In the parable of the mustard seed (Matthew 13:31-32) Jesus compared the kingdom of heaven to a mustard seed, pointing out that from such a tiny seed a large plant would grow. Ordinary black mustard is an annual which grows to three or four feet in height. Young, tender leaves can be eaten in salads and stir-fry recipes. In many places in the South, people boil and eat the large leaves. The condiment mustard is made from the seeds.

Parsley — Wild parsley grew abundantly in the biblical lands and was one of the first herbs to be cultivated. It was a sign of victory and achievement. The ancient Roman athletes wore crowns woven of it. St. Paul refers to this "corruptible crown" in 1 Corinthians 9:25.

Rue (Luke 11:42) and *wormwood* (Revelation 8:10-11) are both bitter herbs, rarely used for culinary purposes, but often grown in gardens for their attractive foliage.

In Praise of Creation — Prayers and Blessings

From the beginning of the Church, Christians prayed for, prayed over, and blessed the created things of the earth.

The following prayer is from the compilation called *The Apostolic Constitutions* written in Syria about A.D. 380. The seventh book of this work contains various forms of prayer for the faithful.

Prayer in Praise of Creation

Blessed art thou, O Lord, King of the ages. Through Christ thou hast created the universe, thou hast given order to the formless world; thou hast separated the waters beneath from the waters above the firmament, though hast breathes into them the breath of life, thou hast established the earth and stretched out the heavens; to every creature thou hast given its appointed place.

Through thy power, O sovereign Lord, the world was established in splendor, the heaven as a vault, lit up with stars, to comfort us in the night; the sun and its light appeared to shine in the day and ripen the harvests, the waxing and waning moon to measure the seasons. They were named the day and the night, and the firmament arose from among the deeps. Thou badest the waters to be gathered together, that the dry land might appear.

The sea's praises who can sing? It is let loose and comes in from the ocean, and thither returns when thou dost forbid it to pass the shore. For thou hast said: its waves shall be broken. There hast thou traced a way for the fishes, great and small, and for the sailors.

And the earth brought forth, in the tapestry of its flowers and the variety of its trees, and the shining stars which give them light follow their unvarying course, never transgressing thy commands. According to thy decrees they rise and set, to mark the seasons and the years regulating man's labour.

Next appeared the various kinds of animals, on land and in the water, and the amphibians; the ordered wisdom of they providence gives to each according to its need; the same power which presided over their creation still watches over the needs of all.

To complete creation according to the orders of thy wisdom, thou madest the creature which is endowed with reason, to inhabit the earth, saying: Let us make man in our image and our likeness. And thou madest him the world of the world, the splendor of splendors. Thou madest his body of the four elements already existing, but his soul thou didst draw from nothing, thou gavest its five senses and the spirit which rules them.

Furthermore, O sovereign Lord, who can worthily tell of the movement of the rain-bearing clouds, of the lightening-flash, the crash of thunder? All things are so ordered as to give every man according to his need, with the greatest variety of temperature.

When man sinned, thou didst withdraw the life promised him in regard, yet thou didst not utterly destroy it, but keepest it veiled for a season. By an other thou didst call him to the new birth. Thou didst tear up the decree of death, thou who restorest life to the dead, through Jesus Christ, our hope. Amen.

Bishop Sarapion's *Prayer-Book*

Near the end of the eighteenth century, a euchology, or prayer-book, was discovered at Mount Athos, providing a liturgical document from early Christian Egypt. The book contains 30 prayers, two of which bear the name of Sarapion of Thmuis, the friend of St. Athanasius. The others are probably by the same author, and were written about A.D. 350. The prayers of this collection belong to the Sunday Office and the eucharistic liturgy, baptism, ordination, the blessing of oils, and funerals. The following prayer is taken from this book.

Prayer for the Fruits of the Earth

Creator of heaven and earth, thou hast adorned the sky with a crown of stars and illuminated it with the sun and the moon, thou hast adorned the earth with its fruits for the service of men, thou hast willed that mankind, created by thee, should rejoice in the bright shining of the sun and moon and be nourished by the fruits of the soil; we beseech thee to send us rains in great abundance and grant to the earth rich harvests and great fertility, because of thy goodness and loving kindness.

Remember those who have recourse to thee; may thy holy and only Catholic Church be honored; hear our prayers and supplications and bless the whole earth through thy only-begotten Jesus Christ, through whom is given to thee the glory and the power, in Holy Spirit, for ever and ever. Amen.

Blessings of Fruits

Various offerings, distinct from the Eucharist, were made by the early Christians, and there were special blessings for each. Besides oil, cheese, and olives, the following were offered and blessed: "grapes, figs, pomegranates, pears, apples, mulberries, peaches, cherries and almonds." Roses and lilies were also often blessed. The following prayer was used about the middle of the fourth century.

Blessing of New Fruits

We thank thee, O God, and we offer thee the firstfruits which thou hast given us to enjoy and hast produced by thy word, bidding the earth bring forth all kinds of fruits, to refresh and feed mankind and all the beasts.

We praise thee, O God, for all these gifts and for all the benefits thou hast bestowed on us, adorning all creation with divers fruits, through thy Son Jesus Christ our Lord, through whom thou art glorified for ever and ever. Amen.

The *Book of Blessings*

In 1989, the *Book of Blessings*, approved for use in the dioceses of the United States of America by the National Conference of Catholic Bishops and confirmed by the Apostolic See, was published, making all the major blessings of the Church available in one convenient collection.

The celebration of blessings should truly contribute to God's praise and glory and should serve to better God's people. From age-old tradition, blessing formularies have centered above all on glorifying God for his gifts, on imploring favors from him, and on restraining the power of evil in this world. As a liturgical action, the celebration of blessings leads the faithful to praise God and prepares them for the principal effect of the sacraments. By celebrating a blessing the faithful can also sanctify various situations and events in their lives.

Ceremonies of blessing have traditionally been held in many parts of the world at planting and harvest time. There are special blessings for animals and even for the tools of man's labor, as well as for the fruits of the harvest. Catholic gardeners who wish to use their gardens as a places of prayer and reflection, in addition to being places of beauty and peace, may wish to ask their local priests about having their gardens blessed. A celebration could be held inviting friends and neighbors to gather for the blessing to celebrate the goodness of God, the Creator.

The following prayer is taken from the new *Book of Blessings*.

Prayer for Seeds

Let us praise God, who plants the seeds and reaps the harvest. Blessed be God for ever.

Today we seek God's blessing on these seeds and the crops they will produce. Christ reminds us that, unless the seed is planted in the earth and dies, it will not yield fruit. As these seeds grow and are cared for, may they be signs of the new life that comes from God. Amen.

Monastery Gardens

Early in the fourth century, the Roman Empire was divided. Constantinople was established as the second capital, and Rome was sacked. The legions withdrew from Britain, leaving it defenseless; Gaul and Spain were overrun. Attila and the Huns ravaged both the Eastern and the Western Empires and at mid-century, Rome was sacked again, this time by the Vandals. By 476, the last Emperor of the West was deposed and the once mighty Empire was destroyed. During the chaotic centuries of the Dark Ages, the Christian Church steadily grew and offered men hope. In the fifth century, monasteries were founded and became storehouses of learning. Their copying and preservation of manuscripts maintained the sum of mankind's knowledge practically intact.

Monasteries were self-sustaining, so agriculture and horticulture were important. The monks preserved the knowledge of plants and herbal lore in addition to the Faith and other knowledge. Plants were exchanged with travelers who sought a night's lodging at the guest house of the monastery. These pilgrims and travelers also brought news and fresh ideas.

In each monastery, there were vegetable plots, vineyards, orchards, and a physic garden of medicinal herbs, as well as a flower garden where flowers were grown to decorate the church. Gardens were tended both inside and outside the walls.

A plan for a monastery drawn in the year 900 is preserved at St. Gall in Switzerland. The plan includes a "paradise" — an open court with a portico, a physic garden with sixteen raised beds for herbs, a hospital with an attendant garden, as well as a garden attached to the school. In addition, the cemetery is a garden planted with fruit and shade trees set in straight rows with the graves between them. The churchyard is a garden, and a large vegetable garden lies next to it with 18 raised beds. There is a house for the gardener because, although all of the monks had to work in the garden, there was usually a full-time professional as well. Descriptions of the twelfth century gardens of Clairvaux Abbey and of Canterbury Cathedral indicate that the monasteries were also well acquainted with the science of garden irrigation.

Vegetable gardens associated with monastic foundations are the earliest type of garden found there. In the sixth century, St. Benedict, one of the great monastic founders, enjoined self-sufficiency in production of vegetables and herbs for his monasteries, and work in the garden for each of its members. The Benedictines preserved the Roman horticultural science and improved gardening techniques throughout the Middle Ages.

At first, the Christian laymen considered flowers in church to be pagan. They associated them with the wreathed Romans and their orgies. The monks, however, sought their beauty to decorate the altars, and on feast days, flowers were woven into chaplets or wreaths for the priest to wear. Slowly, the monks began to "Christianize" and convert the meanings of flowers, giving them associations with Christ, Our Lady, and the saints. For example, the white of the *Lilium candidum* (Madonna lily) symbolized the Virgin's purity; the deep red of the rose with its thorny branches signified Christ's blood.

Each monastery had a quiet, secluded place of simple beauty known as a cloister. This quadrangle was devolved from the classic Roman peristyle and was a place where the monks could walk in seclusion and enjoy the fresh air. In the center of the cloister, there was usually a well, a fountain, or a cistern for water. There might also be a *piscina*, a small pond stocked with fish. A few plants and small fruit or palm trees usually were planted in the cloister.

Herbs in the physic garden were grown as medicines, for repelling vermin, for dye to use in clothing and on the illustrated pages of the manuscripts, and as air fresheners, as well as for flavoring food. Monks skilled in herbal remedies treated not only their fellow monks, but often also the townspeople and those from the nearby manors. Many monasteries had, within or without the walls, a hospital where the infirmarian treated the sick. Herbal lore accumulated, at first based on ancient documents, later collected into hand-copied herbals, and finally printed in book form.

During the time of the Crusades, a period of great religious fervor, garden culture in Europe was greatly enriched. Returning knights brought with them new ideas and plants.

Labyrinths, originally worked out in the pattern of stones in some cathedrals, moved outside. In the labyrinth, penitents moved slowly on their knees, while reciting their prayers at fixed stations. Outside, the labyrinths were made of hedging. The words "labyrinth" and "maze" are sometimes used interchangeably, but many writers agree that the maze was constructed for amusement, had blocked alleys, and was generally formed of lower hedging than the penitential labyrinth.

Tapestries and miniatures, as well as the herbals, display the gardens of the High Middle Ages after the barbaric invasions had ended, and show what pleasure the people took in them. Gardens were places of peace, providing escape from the damp, often smelly, poorly lighted indoor areas of the monasteries and castles.

In this same time period, the borders of illustrated manuscripts often included flowers, sometimes simply for their beauty and sometimes symbolically, illustrating a religious story. Prayer books, called *Books of Hours*, were popular during the Middle Ages, and the illustrations for these contained much floral symbolism. Even the names of these books often alluded to the world of flowers.

The fifteenth century was a time when miniature paintings were popular. Many of these delightful paintings show us how gardens were planned and situated and display the flowers that grew in them. Paintings of the period often used garden scenes, which were filled with religious significance.

One fifteenth-century painting of a "Paradise Garden" (sometimes called a "Mary Garden") shows a seemingly casual garden scene that is filled with Christian symbolism. The enclosed garden symbolized the Virgin Birth. Mary is seated on a cushion reading while her Child humbly plays on the ground. His royal lineage is suggested by the iris, which had a regal connotation. Mary's purity is suggested by white lilies and red roses, symbolizing divine love. The cherry tree signified the joys of heaven. Strawberries, the fruits of righteousness with trefoil leaves suggesting the Trinity, grow near the seated figures of saints Michael and George. Apples on a table symbolize the fall of man and his redemption by Christ. Lilies of the valley in the foreground denote Mary's meekness and purity. Goldfinches perched on the wall were associated with Christ's Passion because of their crimson markings. Other plants favored by medieval Christian symbolists include daisies of innocence, dandelions to symbolize the bitterness of grief and of the Passion, and the plantain, or "waybread," a roadside weed signifying the well-worn path of those seeking Christ.

Today's reader who would like to get the full flavor of a medieval monastery with its attendant gardens would be well advised to read the Brother Cadfael mystery novels of contemporary English novelist Edith Pargeter, writing under the name of Ellis Peters. The fictional Brother Cadfael, an appealing character, is a Benedictine monk and the herbalist for his monastery, Shrewsbury Abbey. Brother Cadfael is a former Crusader and man of the world, and his intelligence and wry humor make him an outstanding character. Several of the books in the series have diagrams, including those showing the various monastery gardens. The description of his herbary and the medicines he concocts are based in reality and show an intimate picture of the life of the twelfth century. His over-900-year-old Benedictine Abbey Church really exists and currently is the subject of a major restoration project. A number of the Brother Cadfael mysteries were produced for television, but although the productions were excellent, they do not include the herbal focus found in the texts.

Make a Medieval Oil Candle

Before the invention of electricity, people made lamps out of various materials. A simple, decorative oil candle can evoke earlier times. Randy, my brother-in-law, brought me one from a Renaissance festival. We adapted the idea with a view to more safety, but as with any project with flammable materials, care should be taken when making or using it. The completed project should be placed up high, out of the way of exploring little hands, and older children should always be warned of the danger of fire, just as you would tell them about candles or matches. For those who live in areas where the lights often go out, this can be a helpful thing to keep around, as well as a pleasant decoration. Use citronella-scented lamp oil and make several to use at outside parties in the summer when the mosquitoes hover; the odor of the citronella will help drive the pests away.

Supplies needed

- heavy glass bottle (clear or light-colored)
- 2 corks to fit the bottle
- ¼" copper tubing
- candlewick
- dried natural materials
- lamp oil
- coping saw, hack saw, or tubing cutter
- ice pick
- large screw (nearly ¼" diameter)
- hammer
- small funnel

Directions

Cut a piece of copper tubing ¾" longer than the length of the cork. Copper is soft and will cut easily with the coping saw, hack saw, or tubing cutter. You can buy copper tubing at the hardware store.

With the ice pick, carefully make a hole from the top to the bottom of the cork. Twist a large screw into the hole to ream it out, then twist the screw back out. You may have to do this from both the top and the bottom if your screw is not long enough to go through the entire cork. This is the only difficult part of this project. Cork is fragile and you don't want to crack it.

When you have made a hole in the cork, use a hammer to gently tap in the copper tubing. The tubing should push into the cork so only the smallest smidgen of tubing sticks out of the bottom of the cork. Tubing should stick out above the cork at least ½".

Cut a piece of candlewick the length of the bottle plus the cork. The one Randy bought me used yarn, but we feel that braided candlewick is safer. Thread the wick through the copper tubing, leaving about ½" above the top of the tubing to light.

If the wick slips too easily through the tubing, you can crimp the top of the tube (after the wick has been pulled up through it) slightly with a pair of pliers or channel locks.

The second cork is to be used to tightly seal your candle when you are not using it. This will prevent evaporation of the oil and help prevent an accidental spill.

Next, push dried natural materials into the bottle, filling it loosely about two-thirds of the way. We used pieces from some old potpourri that had lost its scent. You can gather and dry your own materials, too, using silica gel and your microwave (see instructions for everlastings on page 92). A walk through the closest woods during the fall can yield many naturally dried materials to the observant collector. Senna pods, tiny fir cones, miniature acorns, and the dried tops of wild grasses all have a beauty of their own. Dried cockscomb, rosebuds, and strawflowers add color to the variety of earth tones.

Use a small funnel to add lamp oil to within 2" of the top of the neck of the bottle. (Hint: you can find lamp oil in most hardware stores and some drug and variety stores. Large chain stores like Wal-Mart and K-Mart also sell this oil, along with decorative oil lamps, especially during the Christmas season. The oil comes in clear, unscented, and colored and scented types.)

Some dried materials float, so if it seems as if you need more, you can pour back some of the oil and add more dried materials until it makes a pretty arrangement in the bottle.

Push the long end of the wick down into the bottle. It will tend to float or curl up at the top, but that is okay. The extra length will stay with the level of oil; each time the lamp is lit the wick will need to be pulled up and trimmed. An ice pick may help to push it down a little into the top of your dried materials. Put in the cork and allow the wick to soak up some of the oil. In just a few minutes, your oil candle is ready to light.

If you plan on presenting your oil candle as a gift, do not add the wick mechanism and cork. Instead, tightly cork the bottle with a plain, uncut cork and present the wick mechanism in a small bag tied to the oil candle.

If you like, you can tie a ribbon around the neck of the candle. We liked the shape of a bottle that had a screw-on cap, so we circled the top of this bottle with fabric paint and allowed it to dry; it made a colorful decorative ring at the neck of the bottle and covered the screw threading.

Heavenly, Holy Herbs

For centuries herbs have been used and valued by mankind. Loosely defined, herbs are plants that serve and delight us, offering us a closer rapport with nature. Through the centuries, the definition of this word has changed according to man's relationship with the plant kingdom. With the advent of science and technology, the word has come to have a more limited concept than in earlier history. Today many people consider herbs to be only a few plants used in the kitchen for seasoning.

In recent years there has been a resurgence of interest in botanicals and studies in aromatherapy, naturopathy, and herbal medicine are in vogue.

Although many of today's botanicals were known and used by our pre-Christian ancestors, it was the Church that preserved much Greek and Latin herbal knowledge as scholars in monasteries transcribed ancient documents. In the gardens of these same monasteries, this knowledge was used and given a Christian orientation.

The treatment of human illness became an extension of Church teaching, and Christian healers followed the example of St. Basil, Bishop of Caesarea, in providing care and shelter for the sick.

In the eighth century Charlemagne, King of the Franks and the First Holy Roman Emperor, designated a group of useful plants to be grown in his domain. In the ninth century, the patriarch of Jerusalem sent prescriptions from the East to Alfred the Great, king of the West Saxons.

These cures were written in books called "herbals." Hildegard of Bingen, a twelfth-century German abbess, wrote the *Book of Healing Herbs,* which described a wide range of plants and their uses. Called the "Sybil of the Rhine" for her powers as seeress and prophetess, this flamboyant Benedictine was one of the most remarkable women of the Middle Ages. She also wrote a book on the human body and its ailments.

During the Middle Ages, many plants became associated with Christian saints and martyrs, thus losing their pagan connotations. The rose is a good example. Long associated with Greek and Egyptian gods, the Church fathers rededicated it to the Virgin Mary. Holly, sacred to the druids, became a symbol of Christ's sacrifice, with its spiny leaves recalling the crown of thorns and the red berries symbolizing Christ's blood.

As missionaries spread across Europe, they converted plants as well as people, often using them as teaching tools. The largely illiterate population could not read, but as farmers were familiar with the native plants. Remember St. Patrick's famous example of the shamrock as a symbol of the trinity? Plants were even used as calendars. Those who could not read a calendar could remember that Michaelmas daisies flowered near the time for the feast of St. Michael. The wood sorrell was nicknamed "alleluia" because it bloomed when the gospel response was "alleluia," between Easter and Whitsuntide.

St. John's wort was so named because it bloomed near the feast of John the Baptist. Dedicated to the saint, the Christians continued to hang the plant in doorways to repel evil spirits, just as they did in previous, pagan times.

Priests and monks collected the newly "holy" herb to use in casting out devils.

Even after the advent of modern, laboratory-manufactured pharmaceuticals, botanical medicines and folk healers remained popular among the common people. European immigrants brought their folk medicine to America, where it blended with that practiced by Native Americans for centuries. In rural areas of the Ozark and Appalachian mountains, many people traditionally use botanicals as home remedies. The *curanderos [as]* and native-American medicine men of the Southwest do a brisk business in herbal remedies even today. Some famous *curanderos*, notably Don Pedrito Jaramillo and Nino Fidencia, have been acclaimed as saints by the people who believe it is only a matter of time before the Church canonizes them.

Medical science has proved that there is some truth to many "old wives' tales" of herbal folk medicine. The useful properties of plants such as aloe vera, garlic, mint, and peppers, for example, have been known and used for centuries. Today's scientists have analyzed the chemicals in these plants to explain *why* they work.

Common sense dictates that we should not rely on herbal concoctions to treat serious illness. Today's home gardener, however, can grow a number of plants useful in simple first aid remedies. Additionally, many herbs can be used in the home for cosmetic purposes, to freshen the air and scent clothes in drawers and closets, and to enhance the flavors of food. Most herbs are easy to grow, even in restricted space, so even apartment or town-home dwellers can grow and enjoy botanicals.

Take a trip of fancy and imagine you are a great herbalist in a monastery of the Middle Ages. Enjoy planning a herb garden. It can be as simple as a few pots of herbs on a sunny window sill, or a formal garden plot in a sunny spot of your yard. Your public library and your local garden store have books on the subject for further reference. Plant, harvest, and use some of God's most bountiful gifts — herbs.

Basic Growing Tips

Most herbs prefer a sunny, well-drained location. Soil need not be rich. Many herbs will take over all available space if you don't control them. An easy way to do this is to plant the herbs in large plastic pots with the bottom removed. Sink pots in the ground until only about one inch remains above the soil line.

Herbal Vinegars

Harvesting

Herbs can be used fresh or harvested and dried for later use. Cut herbs for drying in the early morning, bunching the stems. Rinse with cool water. Tie twine around the stems and hang the bunch upside down away from strong light. We hang them over our kitchen counter, where they impart a wonderful scent to the room as they dry. When crispy, work over waxed paper to remove the leaves from the stems. Seal leaves in air-tight jars; stems can be chopped and added to potpourri or thrown back in the garden to compost.

Uses

Many fresh herbs can be used in cooking. Herbal pillows or sachets, herb butter, and herbal vinegars are three other easy ways to use surplus herbs for yourself or for gifts.

Herbal Vinegars

Herbal vinegars are tasty when sprinkled over salads. Use alone or mix with oil. Mix with water to marinate meat, or sprinkle lightly on fish to add flavor.

To make herbal vinegar, rinse fresh herbs well and pick off any less-than-perfect leaves. Push herbs, stems down, into clean bottles. The more herbs you use, the stronger the flavor.

Use a funnel to fill bottle with vinegar (plain or apple) which has been brought to a boil. A pinch of salt may be added if you like.

Cap or cork the bottle and let stand for at least a week before use.

Experiment with different combinations of herbs. One or two hot peppers will spice up your vinegar, and of course you can add peeled cloves of garlic. We have two favorites: dill with thinly sliced lemon peel (minus the white), and garlic with a mixture of purple basil and oregano.

Herb "Butter"

Another easy way to use your home-grown herbs is to make herb "butter." Let a tub of margarine warm to room temperature. Chop your favorite herbs and stir them in the margarine. Refrigerate for several hours to get the full flavor. You can experiment with different combinations to create the flavor you like best. Serve on crackers or bread.

Basil Almond "Butter"

Rinse and chop the basil into the tiniest pieces possible. Chop the almonds into tiny pieces. Stir the basil, almonds, and sugar into the softened margarine. Refrigerate.

Supplies needed — Basil Almond "Butter"

1 cup of margarine, softened

3 almonds, shelled

2 large sweet-basil leaves

½ tsp. sugar

Pillows or Sachets

You can use herbs to make sachets and herbal pillows. Herbal sachets impart a pleasant odor to closets and drawers, and some herbs also repel insects and other household pests. Herbal pillows can help you relax, achieve a restful sleep, or, placed under the pillows of a favorite chair, can help keep your room smelling fresh. These sachets and pillows make inexpensive and welcome gifts.

To make the pillows, sew a bag from leftover lightweight fabric. A 9" square is a good size.

Directions

Place a cup or two of your favorite herbal blend in the pillow and sew the fourth side shut. This forms a thin, limp pillow which you can slide between your regular bed pillow and the case. As you sleep, your head movements on the pillow cause the scent to be released anew.

Sachets are simply small pillows. They are often made of scraps of fancy materials and decorated with small dried flowers or ribbons. A glue gun is

Herbal Pillow

an invaluable tool in attaching the tiny decorations, or you can get exotic and sew on sequins and beads.

The filling for herbal pillows and sachets, like any potpourri, needs a fixative and benefits from the addition of a few drops of essential oil. The most common fixative is powdered orris root; use a teaspoon or more per cup of dried herbs. Sweet orange or lemon are two of the less expensive and more easily available essential oils. You can purchase these items at a herbal shop, or order them by mail from a number of sources. Refer to the index of this book for some mail-order sources.

In a large bowl, mix two or more of your dried herbs with the orris root. Add a few drops of the oil and stir thoroughly. Place the mix in a large zipper-locked plastic bag, shake to distribute the oil, and store in a dark place for about a week. Test to see if the odor pleases you. You can add more oil and re-close for a few more days if your mixture was not strong enough the first time.

When the odor pleases you, stuff your sachets. Sachets containing pennyroyal, lavender, and the

Supplies needed — Sleepytime Pillow

9 tbsp. chamomile flowers

9 tbsp. lemon-balm leaves

3 tbsp. lavender flower

3 tbsp. pennyroyal

1 tbsp. powdered orris root

5 drops rose oil (synthetic)

2 drops tea-tree oil

10 drops lemon oil

5 drops lavender-flower oil

mints repel many household pests, as well as scent your closets. One recipe we like calls for equal amounts of spearmint, oregano, and lemon balm. Add 1 tsp. orris root and three drops of lemon oil per cup of herbs.

Here are recipes for some of our favorite sachets and herbal pillows. Remember, however, that your own preferences can determine the aromas most pleasing to you.

Your sachets and pillows will keep their scent for a long time. Pillows can be stored in zipper-locked plastic bags during the day to extend their life. When they have lost their odor, you can refresh them by adding a few drops of oil directly on the fabric. Another way to refresh the scent is to mix the oils with a few tablespoons of everclear or vodka in a small glass and sprinkle the mixture liberally over the pillow or sachets. Either way, seal them in a plastic bag for a few days before use to allow them to re-cure.

Sleepytime Pillow

This recipe (supplies are listed on the previous page) provides a combination that is soothing and sleep-inducing to many people. Measure dried herbs in heaping tablespoons; measure oil in drops. Mix in a glass or ceramic bowl. Seal in a plastic bag and store in a dark place for one week, shaking daily to mix. Slip loosely stuffed pillow under the regular pillowcase.

Vibrancy Power-Nap Pillow

This recipe can add "oomph" to a power nap. Follow the instructions in the above recipe with the ingredients listed on this page.

Bug-Be-Gone Sachet

This sachet imparts a pleasant odor in drawers and closets and may just help keep them bug free as an added benefit. As above measure in heaping

Supplies needed — Power-Nap Pillow

1 tbsp. lemon-balm leaves

10 tbsp. pennyroyal

5 tbsp. lavender flower

1 tbsp. peppermint

6 tbsp. catnip

1 tbsp. powdered orris root

13 drops sweet-orange oil

12 drops lemon oil

3 drops lavender-flower oil

3 drops ylang-ylang oil

Supplies needed — Bug-Be-Gone Sachet

5 tbsp. lavender flower

5 tbsp. pennyroyal

10 tbsp. spearmint

1 tbsp. powdered- or ground-orris root

12 drops lemon oil

10 drops lavender flower-oil

Supplies needed — Herbal Pot-Holder

cotton-print fabric

sewing machine and thread

scissors

cotton batting or pillow
  stuffing

dried spices such as:

stick cinnamon

whole allspice

star anise

whole cloves

bay leaves

pickle spice mix

Supplies needed — Herbal Shoe Stuffers

3 cups cedar chips

½ cup lavender flowers

2 tbsp. whole cloves

20 drops sweet orange oil
  (or substitute lemon oil)

tablespoons and drops, mix in non-metal container, and cure in a plastic bag, shaking daily to distribute ingredients. Stuff in small cloth pillows about 2" or 3" square, or purchase ready-made small drawstring bags.

Herbal Pot-Holder

Make an herbal pot-holder which will softly scent your kitchen each time you use it and in between times, too.

Sew a pillow about 8" square. Crumble some of your dried spices in a small bowl. Experiment until you have a blend that pleases you. Stuff your pillow with batting and add one to two tablespoons of the dried spice mix. If you like, you can use a long running stitch to quilt across your pot holder.

Herbal Shoe Stuffers

You can make a refreshing blend of deodorizing herbs and spices and make shoe stuffers to keep your shoes smelling sweet.

In a large bowl, stir together the ingredients listed.

Make sachet bags 2 ½" wide by 6" long of lightweight cotton cloth. Stuff them tightly with the above mix. Place one sachet inside each shoe. Hint: you can purchase cedar chips at the pet store; it is often used for bedding for small animals.

Twenty Top Herbs and Tips for Their Use

Here are 20 of our favorite herbs to grow and to enjoy. Most are easily grown in the majority of climates in the United States. A number of uses for each are given.

Aloe Vera — A first aid kit in a leaf! This most useful of plants prefers a sunny location with dry, sandy soil. It grows well in a pot on the windowsill and provides instant relief for minor burns and cuts. Simply slice off a piece of the leaf and squeeze out the sticky juice to apply to your wound. It also stops the pain and stinging of sunburn.

Basil—The reputation of this plant has alternated between good and bad for centuries. Some praised it; some damned it. It was once associated with a legendary reptile called the basilisk, whose look or breath could kill you. It was also known as a symbol of love and a protection against witches. Medicinally, it helps prevent flatulence, and most cooks count it as a staple. The common or sweet basil, purple basil, cinnamon basil, and lemon basil are all excellent for herbal butters and vinegars.

Bay — With its glossy green leaves, the bay laurel grows more like a shrub than a tree, and will live happily in a large pot for many years. Cooks treasure the leaves, and a single leaf makes a flavorful addition to stews and many bean dishes. Sprays or wreaths made of the leaves can sweeten and freshen the air in the home, and although humans usually appreciate the odor, many bugs dislike it. Place a single leaf or two in the closet or drawer as a pleasant and simple sachet.

Catnip is one of the mint cousins, and can be used as any mint. During the Middle Ages, it was given to the knights to make them more aggressive, but today the tea is used as a calming force and can help sooth a mild headache. Cat lovers beware! This herb generally acts on felines the way it was supposed to act on the knights. We grow our catnip in hanging baskets to prevent the cats from destroying our herb beds. Save old panty hose and use double or triple layers of this material to tie dried catnip leaves into balls for cat toys. Or sew dried catnip in small pillows for your feline friends. During the growing season, our cats enjoy chewing one or two of the fresh leaves daily.

Cutting celery — Wild celery was used as a remedy for flatulence and rheumatism, and sometimes recommended for dropsy and hysteria. In the seventeenth century, Italian gardeners developed the stalk celery we know today. Plants sold as "cutting celery" are grown for their leaves which are dried and used in soups, stews, and herb salt.

Dill — Although best known today in its flavoring of pickles, a side dish that came to America from Germany, dill was known and used medicinally by the Egyptians over 5,000 years ago. Its name comes from the Old Norse word "*dilla*," which means "to lull," and dill was used as "gripe water" to relieve digestive discomfort. It was also used as a cure for hiccups. Today's uses are primarily culinary, and dill mixes well with vinegar, egg, and potato dishes.

Garlic — Research shows that garlic has antiseptic properties and helps to reduce cholesterol and prevent heart disease.

Buy a fresh bulb of garlic at the grocery store and carefully separate the cloves, trying to keep some roots on each section. Plant the root end-down in a pot or in the garden. Garlic repels some garden pests, and roses like to have garlic as a bedmate. Garlic can be harvested after it has bloomed and the tops have died down, but its leaves are useful year-round. With a sharp scissors, clip one or two leaves from the garlic plant. Rinse well and cut into tiny pieces. Stir into soft margarine for a delicious garlic butter, or use in your favorite soup for a mild garlic flavor.

Ginger — This is another plant easy to grow from grocery-store stock. Buy a plump piece of ginger root in the produce department and plant in a large pot or bucket of sand. Beautiful tall leaves will shoot up and within a few weeks the root will begin to enlarge. When you need a piece of ginger for cooking a special dish, dig down around the root and slice off a piece for kitchen use. Peelings and leftovers can be dried for use in potpourri. Chew a piece of the root to soothe a sore throat.

Lemon balm — This beautiful, hardy plant has been used for centuries for its soothing medicinal qualities and its aromatic properties. A tea made from fresh or dried leaves soothes menstrual cramps, relieves insomnia, and acts as a mild sedative. Volatile oil from the leaves is used in the manufacture of perfumes and cosmetics. Dried leaves are a good additive to potpourri. Feeling a little down? Tie a handful of lemon balm leaves in a double layer of old hose. Place the hose under the water stream and draw a warm bath. The soothing, refreshing odor is sure to revive your spirits.

Lemongrass — This is a large plant but it can be grown in pots. It may be difficult to find in some of the colder areas of the United States, so if you can't locate it at your local nursery or herb shop, try the oriental grocery store. If you have to resort to the grocery store, but the freshest available. Most roots will have probably been removed, but as long as there are root bulblets it should grow. Cut pieces of the grass to impart a delicate lemon flavoring to sauces or oriental cooking (remove pieces before serving.) It dries well for use in potpourri. We use it for our hair. In a medium saucepan of water, bring to a boil five to 10 two-inch pieces of lemon grass. Cover and let stand until cool. Use as a final rinse when washing hair to remove soap dullness and impart a silky shine and a delicate fragrance.

Mint — Spearmint, peppermint, and some of the more exotic mints such as orange or chocolate mint are all easily grown. The mints like water, so a good place for them is near the water faucet. Teas made from these mints help to settle a stomach and, added to other teas, make a refreshing drink. Boil a generous handful of the leaves of any of these mints in two quarts of water to use as an addition to fruit punch for a party. In a one-gallon glass jar, place a handful of mint leaves and two or three tea bags. Set the jar in a sunny place for several hours to make delicious mint flavored sun tea.

Oregano — Will the real oregano please stand up? A number of plants go by the names oregano and marjoram. Try the one that is advised as the easiest to grow in your area. All are prolific and, like their cousins the mints, will take over where you let them. Any of these plants is useful in cooking. Use fresh or dry in pizza or pasta sauces. After the leaves are harvested, save the stems to throw on a barbecue fire. We also use our prolific oregano as one of the mainstays of our herbal pillows and potpourris, as well as in herbal vinegars.

Parsley — Parsley was used by the Greeks to crown victors at the Isthmian Games and to decorate tombs. The Romans used it as a food and consumed it in quantity to discourage intoxication and to counter strong odors. Easily grown, parsley can be dried but is best used fresh. Use as a garnish which can be eaten to sweeten the breath or chop and add to soups and stews. Our favorite is with red potatoes. Boil potatoes until tender, changing the water once to remove any bitterness. When tender, strain off water and fork open the potatoes. Add margarine, garlic powder, chopped parsley and a small amount of salt. Add enough milk to cover bottom of pan about one-half-inch deep. Stir together and serve.

Peppers — More and more, modern science has come to value the capsicum, which makes peppers hot. Any of the small hot peppers is suitable for the home gardener. When the plant begins to produce peppers, remember that the more you harvest, the more the plant will grow. Pack rinsed whole peppers tightly in a small empty bottle. Add one-half teaspoon of salt. Use a funnel to fill the jar with boiling vinegar. Cap and let stand for at least a week for hot pepper sauce for greens.

When peppers turn red, string them on thread to dry. Strings can be tied to a curtain rod ring and finished with a small bow for a decorative accent or dried peppers may be crushed for use in cooking.

Pennyroyal — Housewives and dogs love this low-growing member of the mint family because mice, fleas, ants, and flies don't.

This spreading herb can be planted in the yard in several places to help repel pests. Its dried leaves make an interesting additive to herb pillows. Although used for culinary purposes in some cultures, and medicinally in some others, pennyroyal should definitely *not* be taken by pregnant women or anyone with kidney problems.

Pineapple sage — Eat a flower today! Pineapple sage has a wonderful odor and the leaves make a good addition to potpourri. The tiny scarlet flowers make an interesting and colorful addition to salads, giving even the humblest a gourmet look.

Rose geranium — All the scented geraniums (pelargoniums) are valued as aromatics and used in aromatherapy. The flowers can be tossed in a salad and the dried leaves are wonderful for potpourris and sachets. These are good pot growers. In the winter, pots can be brought inside and placed where brushing against them will scent the entire room — they summer outdoors in a sunny location. Use fresh leaves tied in hose for a refreshing bath, or bury them in layers of sugar in a jar for several days to make flavored sugar.

Roses are useful in medicines and cooking as well as for their beauty. A number of beautiful and interesting miniature varieties have been developed so even apartment dwellers can grow roses. Rose "hips," or fruits, are a good source of vitamins. Rose petals can be made into jellies or syrups, and are the basis for most potpourris. Keep a box on top of your refrigerator and as each rose finishes its bloom, put it in the box to dry.

Rosemary — In ancient Greece, students wore sprigs of rosemary in their hair to aid their memory, and the plant is a symbol of remembrance. The tiny leaves are a staple in the kitchen. Soak dried stems in water and throw on barbecue coals for flavorful smoke.

Sweet violets — Although this beautiful little plant has been known and revered by herbalists since before the time of Christ, most of its claims to medicinal benefits have not been validated by modern science. They make pretty floral accents to the shady side of the herb garden, and you can candy the flowers for delicate cake decorations. Beat one egg white with a fork until frothy. Paint the violets with the egg white using a small, clean paint brush. Gently cover with granulated sugar and place on a plate of sugar to dry.

Grow a Rosemary Christmas Tree

Decorate a tiny Christmas tree of rosemary with miniature ornaments. It's a perfect accent for a desk at the office or a fragrant and thoughtful gift for a shut-in or hospital patient.

In the spring, purchase a small pot of rosemary for each tree you want to make. At home, repot the plant into a larger pot; a 6" pot is a good size for a tree that should grow to about 12" tall by Christmas. Insert a thin, wooden dowel about 18" long in the center of the pot; about 12" of the dowel should stick up above the dirt. Using green twist ties, loosely attach the center two or three stems of the rosemary plant to the dowel. Keep the pot in a sunny place, watering as needed. Each month, trim the rosemary as needed, working it into a Christmas tree shape. As the center stems grow taller, you can train them against the dowel by using more twist ties. Save the trimmings to dry for other projects. By Christmas, you should have a well-shaped, bushy tree.

Just before presenting your tree, decorate it with miniature ornaments. You can make garlands for the tree by stringing tiny beads on thread. Other tiny ornaments can be purchased or crafted from Sculpey or other oven-hardening clay.

What Is a Weed?

The word "weed" is of unknown origin and is a relative term. In the most widely accepted sense, a weed is any troublesome and useless plant growing on cultivated ground to the injury of the crop or vegetation desired. The Oxford dictionary defines the term as a "herbaceous plant not valued for use or beauty, growing wild and rank, and regarded as cumbering the ground and hindering the growth of superior vegetation." Shakespeare refers to such plants as lacking "both beauty and utility."

But in another sense, any plant growing where it is not wanted is regarded as a weed. In this sense there are no species of weed, because a plant might be a weed in one place and not a weed in another. Even a corn plant growing in a wheat field would be a weed. The United States Department of Agriculture defines a weed as "an unwanted plant, or a plant out of place. " In the popular sense, a weed signifies a plant that is more or less useless, irrespective of where it grows. The poet Ralph Waldo Emerson wrote, "And what is a weed? A plant whose virtues have not been discovered."

The word used in such phrases as "widow's weeds," is derived from an Anglo-Saxon root meaning "to weave," and is not related to weed in the sense of an unwanted or obnoxious plant. Formerly, clothes in general were called "weeds."

Incense: Pray-and-Sniff

In ancient times, people believed that whatever delighted the human senses must also be pleasing to the gods. They felt that through the burning of sacrificial offerings — and the ascension of the smoke — their gifts were transported into the realm of the divinity.

In those days, modern sanitation was unknown and bathing was a luxury. No wonder incense, perfumes, and other sweet-smelling items were popular.

In recent times, science has discovered smell is the only sense wired directly to the limbic system, sometimes called the "old mammalian brain. "That's what regulates vital autonomic functions, biological rhythms, and basic instincts. In other words, our sense of smell affects the source of our most powerful emotions.

The earliest recorded use of incense is found in Egyptian hieroglyphics. About 1500 B.C., Queen Hatshepsut sent a fleet to what is now part of northern Somalia to acquire frankincense and myrrh tree seedlings, the two "perfumes of the gods." When the tomb of Tutankhamen (c. 1340 B.C.) was opened in the early twentieth century, the air inside still smelled of myrrh.

In addition to the Ten Commandments and other instructions, Moses brought two recipes down from Mount Sinai. These were for sacred incense made with frankincense and sacred anointing oils with a myrrh base (Exodus 30:22-38).

The Magi brought gifts of gold, frankincense, and myrrh to the Messiah. All were rare and costly commodities in the ancient world. Both frankincense and myrrh are aromatic gum resins, or dried tree sap. Because the trees were scarce and difficult to transplant, and harvesting was a laborious process, the resins were very valuable. Around the time of Christ, a pound of frankincense cost more than the equivalent of $500 in today's currency; a pound of the choicest myrrh was as much as eight to 10 times that amount.

Modern scholars believe that the use of incense was not a part of the earliest Christian worship for two reasons. Its pagan connotations left a bad taste in Christian mouths. During the Roman persecution, Christians were ordered to offer incense before an image of the emperor or other pagan deities. Those who capitulated were called "*thurificati*," after the "*thurible*" or censer in which incense was burned. Additionally, much of the early Christian worship was held in secret and the strong odor of incense could have brought danger, persecution, or death to the worshippers.

After the time of the persecutions, incense began to be used in Christian celebrations and its use continues today. The rising smoke suggests the ascent of the prayers of the faithful gathered there. The ritual censing of church objects symbolizes sanctification — to sanctify is to make holy. The incensing of the worshippers not only implies sanctification, but also celebrates participation in the liturgical ceremony.

Herbal Lore in Christian Tradition

For centuries, herbs have been associated with Christian traditions and myths. References to others are abundant in the Scripture. Here are some of the popular Christian legends and myths associated with a variety of plants familiar to home gardeners today.

Agrimony (hemp) was also known as "holy rope" because it was named after the rope with which the Savior was bound.

Almonds — In Numbers 17:8, we read that Moses went into the tabernacle of witness and found that the rod of Aaron had budded and brought forth buds, and bloomed blossoms, and yielded almonds. This rod was said to have reached Rome, where it became the staff of the Pope. In the Tannhauser legend, it became the symbol of forgiveness when it miraculously greened. Almonds have grown abundantly in the Holy Land since biblical times and were used as models for decoration on the candlesticks in the Temple, as well as on currency during the time of the Maccabees.

Angelica— The plant was originally associated with a pagan festival, but after the introduction of Christianity it became linked in the popular mind with some archangelic patronage and associated with the festival of the Annunciation. According to one legend, angelica was revealed by an angel in a dream to cure the plague. Another explanation of the name is that it blooms on the day of St. Michael the Archangel (old calendar) and thus is a preservative against evil spirits and witchcraft. It was held in such esteem that it was called the "root of the Holy Ghost."

Apples were central and northern Europe's most important cultivated crop at the time of the discovery of America. Early in the settlement of this country, apple trees were planted by the Pilgrims on an island in Boston harbor, by the Dutch in New York, and by Jesuit missionaries passing through the valley of the St. Lawrence River.

Avens— (*Geum urbanum*, herb bennet, wild rye, goldy star) —This herb was called the "blessed herb" because it was worn as an amulet to ward off evil spirits. An herbal printed in 1491 states that "Where the root is in the house, Satan can do nothing and flies from it." The original name may have been St. Benedict's Herb, from the legend of the time a monk presented the saint with a goblet of poisoned wine which, after being blessed by the saint, shattered. In medieval days, the plant's graceful trefoil leaf and the five golden petals of the flowers symbolized the Holy Trinity and the five wounds of Our Lord.

Balm (lemon balm) — A spirit of balm combined with lemon peel, nutmeg, and angelica root enjoyed a great reputation under the name of Carmelite water, probably after the convent where it was first used extensively. The water was deemed useful to cure nervous headaches and neuralgic affections.

Barberry — Among the Italians, the barberry bears the name of holy thorn, because it is thought to have formed part of the crown of thorns made for Our Savior. There is another superstition that the crown was made of buckthorn. Yet another tradition held the hawthorne tree as the bush which furnished the Crown of Thorns.

Basil — Legend tells that St. Helen had a vision in which she learned that she could find the true cross in a place where the air was sweet with perfume. She is said to have discovered it in a patch of basil.

Bay leaves come from the laurel tree, a small evergreen with a long historical and mythological background. Greatly esteemed by the Greeks and the Romans, it was used to crown heroes. From their word for laurel berry (*bacca lauri*) comes our word "baccalaureate." Herbalists in early days said the leaves soothed in baths, gave strength in potions, and, tucked behind the ear, kept one sober. It was valued in the Middle Ages as a charm against witches and devils. The leaves of this evergreen were used to ornament churches well into the last century, especially at Christmas time.

Lady's bedstraw (*Galium verum*), also known as Our Lady's bedstraw or cheese rennet. This plant, by Christian legend, was one of the cradle herbs, or plants that were in the hay at the manger in Bethlehem. It was used in stuffing beds or mattresses in Europe.

Wood betony (*Stachys betonica* or *Betonica officinalis*) was cultivated in the physic gardens of the apothecaries and the monasteries because it was considered throughout the centuries as a panacea for all ills. In addition to its medical powers, it was endowed in the popular mind with power against evil spirits and so was planted in churchyards and hung about the neck.

According to Erasmus, it "sanctified those that carried it about them" and was also "good against fearful visions" and an efficacious means of "driving away devils and despair."

Blackberries have grown wild in the temperate regions from earliest times, and have appeared in many legends. Possibly Moses' burning bush was a blackberry bush. Some legends hold that Christ's crown of thorns may have come from the blackberry and that is why the devil hates blackberries.

Borage was sometimes called herb-of-gladness. According to Pliny, borage in wine drove away sadness and sorrow and brought courage. Therefore, Crusaders leaving for the wars were given a stirrup cup with borage leaves floating in it. Bracken (*Pteris aquilina*) is sometimes called brake or female fern. The minute spores of this fern were reputed to confer invisibility on their possessor if gathered at the only time when they were said to be visible, i.e., on St. John's Eve at the precise moment at which the saint was born.

Broom (*Cytisus scoparius*) by an old tradition was cursed by the Virgin when the Holy Family were fleeing into Egypt, because the crackling of their ripe pods risked drawing attention of the soldiers of Herod. The bad connotations of the plant apparently disappeared, however, because the flowering tops were used later for house decorations at the Whitsuntide festival. The plant was much used in heraldry. A prince of Anjou assassinated his brother and seized his kingdom, but after being overcome by remorse he made a pilgrimage to the Holy Land, in expiation. Every night of his journey, he scourged himself with a brush made of this plant, and adopted it as his badge in perpetual memory of his repentance. St. Louis of France continued the use of this token, and founded a special order that wore a collar containing this flower along with the motto "*Exaltat humiles*" ("He exalteth the lowly").

Carob is colloquially known as "St. John's bread," in the belief that it was the "locust" recorded in the Bible as being eaten by John the Baptist in the wilderness. Actually, it is the pod and not the seed of the tree which is ground into a powder and used as a more wholesome substitute for chocolate. It also probably corresponds with the husks of the Prodigal Son parable. The seed is said to have been the original jewelers' carat weight.

Chervil has a long-standing medical reputation. Because of its reputed rejuvenating qualities, the herb came to symbolize resurrection and new life. In parts of Europe a soup made of chervil is eaten on Holy Thursday in commemoration of the resurrection.

Chestnuts, in Christian symbolism, denote chastity. In Tuscany, they were eaten on St. Simon's Day and on the Feast of St. Martin, when they were also distributed to the poor.

Christmas Rose (*Helleborus niger*) — The legend of the Christmas rose tells that an angel's wings swept the ground in order to provide a gift for a poor girl, who was weeping because she had no gift to place beside those brought by the shepherds to the manger at Bethlehem.

Clary (*Salvia verbenaca*) was sometimes known as *Oculus Christi*, or Christ's Eye, because of its use in clearing eyesight. The seeds, when moistened, produce a soft, tasteless mucilage and this was put into the eye to remove dust or other obstructions.

Cowslip (*Primula veris*) is commonly called herb Peter or Our Lady's keys in Europe. The pendent flowers of the plant suggest a bunch of keys, the emblem of St. Peter. In Norse mythology, the flower was dedicated to Freya, the Key Virgin, and in northern Europe the idea of dedication to the goddess was transferred to the Virgin Mary. Cowslip flowers have been used to make wine and in a number of home remedies, one of which prompted an old herbal writer to remark with some disdain, "Some women we find, sprinkle ye floures of cowslip w' whyte wine and after still it and wash their faces w' that water to drive wrinkles away and to make them fayre in the eyes of the worlde rather than in the eyes of God, Whom they are not afrayd to offend."

Dandelion, so common in America, was called "priest's crown" in the Middle Ages. When all the puffy white seeds have floated away, all that remains is the disk on which they were placed which resembled, to the common man of the Middle Ages, the shorn head of the priest.

Elder (*Sambucus nigra*): It was a common mediaeval belief that Judas was hanged on an elder tree. In the "Vision of Piers Plowman," written in the middle of the fourteenth century, Langland writes: "Judas he japed with Jewen silver/ And sithen an eller hanged hymselve." Another old tradition was that the Cross of Calvary was made of it, although an equally prevalent English tradition holds that the cross was formed of boxwood.

"Bour tree-Bour tree: crooked rong
Never straight and never strong;
Ever bush and never tree
Since our Lord was nailed on thee."

Because of these old traditions, the elder became the emblem of sorrow and death. A host of superstitious fancies grew up about the tree in all parts of Europe that remained among common country folk for centuries. In Russia, the trees were believed to drive away evil spirits; the Bohemians used it to take away fever. Sicilians kept sticks of the wood to kill serpents and drive away robbers. In England, a twig of it tied into at least three knots and carried in the pocket was a charm against rheumatism. A cross made of elder was hung on the stables to keep all evil from the animals. An elder bush trimmed into the form of a cross was planted on a new-made grave, and if it blossomed, the soul of the person lying beneath it is happy. Green branches were also buried in the grave to protect the dead from witches and evil spirits, and in some parts it was customary for the hearse driver to carry a whip made of elder wood. Another old tradition advised that on Bertha Night (January 6) the devil goes about with special virulence, so persons are recommended to remain inside a circle of elderberries gathered on St. John's night.

Jew's Ears is a large fungus often found on the elder (*Hirneola auricula Judar*). The name is a corruption of "Judas's ear." The purplish fungus was used medicinally and is edible.

In spite of its sad and sorrowful legends, the *elder* is a very useful plant. It was used medicinally and for making wine and jelly. Elderflower water was a common toilet article thought to keep the skin fair and remove freckles and pimples. It was used, mixed with peppermint, as a cure for influenza. During World War I, elderflower ointment was used on wounded horses. Additionally, elderflowers were used in much delicate cookery in England and were added to the posset of the Christening feast.

Elecampane (*Inula helenium*), also known as wild sunflower or velvet dock, was known to the ancient writers on agriculture and natural history. In the beginning of the seventh century, St. Isidore named it *Inula quam Alam rustici vocant*. It was greatly esteemed by the monks as a cordial and was considered to help digestion, cause mirth, fasten the teeth, and cure sciatica. It was also candied and eaten as a sweetmeat, and in eighteenth-century London was mixed with sugar as a remedy for asthma, whooping cough, and piles. In the United States it was used for diseases of the skin.

Eyebright (*Euphrasia officinalis*) — The poet Milton relates how the Archangel Michael ministered to Adam after the fall:

> " . . . to nobler sights
> Michael from Adam's eyes the film removed,

> Then purged with euphrasine and rue
> His visual orbs, for he had much to see."

Fennel — This herb, together with St. John's wort and other herbs, was hung over doors on Midsummer's Eve to warn off evil spirits. It was also used as a condiment to the salt fish that was so often consumed during Lent because of its carminative, or digestion-stimulating, properties.

The *sycamore fig* (*Ficus sycamorus*), a popular shade tree in Egypt and Syria, bears an edible fruit similar to the common fig. In the sacred dramas of the Middle Ages, the tree was used to represent the fig tree into which Zaccheus climbed and that in which by an old legend the Virgin Mary on her journey into Egypt had hidden herself and the infant Jesus. Figs are one of the most ancient fruits and fossil figs have been dated to 65 million years ago. There are many references to figs in the Bible, the most familiar being Adam and Eve sewing fig leaves together for clothing. Two hundred cakes of figs were included in the presents that Abigail offered David. St. Augustine was sitting beneath a fig tree wrestling with some doubts about statements in the Scriptures when he heard the tree speak to him in a child's voice instructing him to read again. He did, and came to believe.

Filbert — The name of the popular filbert nut is the corruption of the name of a Norman saint, Philibert, whose saint's day coincided with the time the nuts ripen.

Flax (*Linum usitatissimum*) is today more commonly known as linseed. Its cultivation goes back to remote history, and the fine linen mentioned in the Bible has been proved to have been spun from flax. The knowledge of spinning this linen extends back into Old Testament times, and in New Testament times it formed the clothing of the Savior in the tomb where Joseph of Arimathaea laid Him.

Garlic (*Allium sativum*) — The legend of this most popular herb comes from the Mohammedan, rather than the Christian, tradition. When Satan stepped out from the Garden of Eden after the fall of man, garlic sprang up from the spot where he placed his left foot and onion from that where his right foot touched. The plant was one of the main ingredients of "four thieves vinegar," which was used in France as a protection against the plague of 1722. The vinegar originated with four thieves who confessed that while protected by the liberal use of this aromatic vinegar during the plague, they plundered the dead bodies of the plague victims with complete security.

During an outbreak of infectious fever in London in the early 1800s, the French priests who constantly used garlic in their food visited the worst cases with impunity, while the English clergymen caught the infection easily. Medical research since the 1920s has shown that garlic does have significant antibiotic activity. Additionally, garlic may help to prevent cardiovascular disease as it aids in reducing cholesterol, preventing blood clots, and lowering blood pressure. One of the smaller alliums, or garlics, called "*ajo macho*," is revered by Hispanics of the New World as a good luck charm said to increase financial prospects; an old legend says it was found growing at Calvary.

Gourds have been symbolic in many religions. It was the primal egg of the Hindus. The Hebrews saw that Jonah's gourd, "which came up in a night and perished in a night," taught him compassion. Gourds were used to point the moral of rapid growth and quick decay, and they illustrate many religious emblems. In Christian symbolism, a gourd is the attribute of Christ, St. James, and the Archangel Raphael. The Holy Child of the Atocha is always pictured with a water gourd from which he dispensed an unending stream of water to the prisoners of the Moors.

Goutweed (*Aegopodium podagraria*) is commonly known as goatweed, herb gerard, pigweed, bishopsweed, or ground elder. It was called bishopsweed and bishopswort because it was frequently found near old ecclesiastical ruins. The monks of the Middle Ages cultivated it as a healing herb. It was called herb gerard because it was dedicated to the saint who was often invoked to cure the gout, against which the herb was chiefly employed.

Grape — The grape is one of the oldest cultivated plants, and fossilized grape leaves about 70 million years old have been discovered. Grapes were the vines that Adam, Eve, and Noah planted. In the Bible we read that the Israelites sent spies to report on the promised land of Canaan; they returned with the legendary bunch of *eschol* that needed two men to carry it. The surprised Israelites, used to small Egyptian grapes, were pleased to find such largesse in the barren and sandy dessert. Moses exempted vineyard planters from military service and wrote a law prohibiting pruning and harvesting of vines in sabbatical years. There was a vine sculpted from gold and grapes made from precious stones on the eastern wall of the old temple in Jerusalem. Clusters of grapes were used on ancient coins. The grape went on to become one of the most important symbols of Christianity. Jesus said, "I am the true vine and my father is the husbandman." Vines decorated the catacombs.

Wine is used in the sacrament of Communion. Monasteries in many countries have always played an important part in grape growing. Grapes were among the first cultivated crops planted by the Franciscan and Jesuit fathers in New Spain. The early missions in California were active grape producers, and almost all of the Rio Grande Valley was planted to vineyards by the middle of the 1800s.

Heartsease (*Viola tricolor*), or wild pansy, is called in many old herbals "*Herba Trinitatis.*" Old writers dedicated this delicate little flower to the Trinity because each flower had three colors in it.

Holly (*Ilex aquifolium*) — A Christmas favorite, legends regarding the holly abound both in pagan and Christian literature. From very early days in the history of the British islands, holly was gathered in great quantities for Yuletide decorations, both in the Church and in homes, and the old carols are full of allusions to it. The Romans sent boughs of holly with other gifts to their friends during the Saturnalia, a custom the early Christians adopted. A later edicts forbade Christians to decorate their houses at Christmas with green boughs at the same time as the pagan celebrations. Old Church calendars mark Christmas Eve "*templa exornantur*" (churches are decked) and evergreens, especially holly, seem to have survived early prohibitions as customary Christmas decorations. An old legend declared that holly sprang up in the footsteps of Christ when He trod the earth and the thorny leaves and scarlet berries, the color of blood, came to symbolize Christ's sufferings. From this, the plant is often called "Christ's Thorn" in northern countries of Europe.

Iris (*Pseudacorus*), *Fleur de Lis* — Early in the sixth century, the Frankish King Clovis, faced with defeat in battle, was induced to pray for victory to the God of his Christian wife, Clothilde. He conquered, became a Christian, and replaced the three toads on his banner with three irises, because the iris was known as the Virgin's flower.

Lady's mantle (*Alchemilla vulgaris*) — In the Middle Ages, this plant, like so many others, became associated with the Virgin Mary. The lobes of the leaves seemed to resemble the scalloped edges of a mantle.

Lavender — All the ancients loved and used lavender, although it did develop an association with snakes. During the Middle Ages, it became associated with the Virgin Mary and represented her purity and virtue. Lavender was burned on the great bonfires of Europe kindled on St. John's Eve to drive away evil spirits.

Leeks — In 640, there was a battle between the Welsh and the Saxons. St. David advised the Welsh to pick some leeks from a nearby garden and wear them in their caps so that they would be able to identify each other. The Welsh won a great victory and ever since have worn leeks in their caps on St. David's Day, March 1.

Lettuce — The slang use of the word "lettuce" to mean "money" may go way back to a story told about Pope Sixtus V, who once sent a salad to an impoverished lawyer, a friend of his. The man had determined to ask the pope for aid, but fell ill on the way. The pope sent word that he would send a salad that would cure him. Sixtus dispatched a messenger with a basket of lettuce. When the lawyer opened the heads, he found them filled with money.

Lily of the Valley, also called Mary's tears, along with roses, sweet flag, sweet woodruff, boxwood, and broom, as well as other white flowers, were made into garlands on Whitsunday in England. The young people made the garlands, carried them through the streets of the village, and laid them on the altar in the church.

Madonna lily — In the early days of the Church, this flower was dedicated to the Madonna, probably because its delicate whiteness was considered a symbol of purity. It is traditionally used in Europe in the celebrations of the Visitation of the Blessed Virgin.

Maidenhair fern — The plant known in old Iceland as "Freyje's hair" became known as Our Lady's hair and Maria's fern. Its scientific name indicates that in ancient times it was dedicated to Venus.

Mandrake — Magical and mysterious properties have always been attributed to the mandrake, and fantastic tales have been told of the dangers of obtaining the root. Some scholars today believe that the vinegar offered to Christ on the cross was actually mandragora wine. A pain-killing drink of mandragora was often given to those who were to be crucified. This Roman wine, whose ingredients included both mandragora and myrrh, was known as morion, or "death wine." During the Middle Ages, monks used mandragora wine as an anesthetic. When St. Benedict amputated the leg of Emperor Henry II, he placed the emperor on a pillow containing mandragora to relieve the pain of the operation. By the thirteenth century the plant became more popular as an aphrodisiac than as an anesthetic, and the best plants for this use were supposed to be gathered from the grave of an innocent man hanged for rape. In the writings of Hildegard of Bingen, she mentions that depression and lovesickness are helped by mandrake.

One of the accusations of witchcraft alleged at the trial of Joan of Arc was that she possessed a mandrake root that she carried close to her. In some countries the best time to gather this root was on the Feast of St. John the Baptist. St. Thomas More described a strange glowing light the root was supposed to give off at night: "Such rank and deadly lustre dwells, / As in those hellish fires that light / The mandrake's charnel leaves at night."

Sweet marjoram — On St. Luke's Day, single women were advised to mix marjoram, marigolds, thyme, and a little wormwood with honey and vinegar. They then were to anoint themselves with this mixture when they went to bed and repeat the following lines in order to dream of their future husband: "St. Luke, St. Luke, be kind to me/ In dreams let me my true love see." Marjoram was also associated with death, and a good growth of this plant on a grave meant the soul of the person there was at rest.

Marigold — This is also called "Mary's Gold." This is said to be because of the golden color of the flowers and the fact that they were used to adorn Marian altars.

Marsh marigold — This plant was "Christianized" and dedicated to the Virgin Mary during the Middle Ages, and offered to her in the springtime. Originally, it was one of the plants hung above the doors by the pagans as a good luck charm and was woven into wreaths by the worshippers of Baal.

Mugwort — This plant was called St. John's plant in the Middle Ages because it was believed that St. John the Baptist wore a girdle of it in the wilderness. On his feast, girls made a crown from its sprays and wore it to prevent evil possession. Gathered on St. John's Eve, it protected against disease and misfortunes all year.

Olive — The olive is the emblem of peace, its branch carried by the dove, and linked with the rescue of Noah and his family on Mount Ararat. When Adam died, three olive seeds were placed in his mouth and from them grew a cypress, a cedar, and an olive tree. Moses' tears kept the trees alive for the 40 years in the wilderness, and eventually they grew into a single tree, under which King David wept for his sins. The tree was preserved by Solomon as a relic in his famous Temple. Gethsemane, on the Mount of Olives, means literally "olive oil press." In some parts of Italy, an olive branch is still hung above the door of a new house to keep the devil out. Olive oil was used to light holy lamps in tabernacles, as mentioned in Exodus 27:20, and as a base for expensive perfumes. In depicting the Annunciation, early painters represented the Angel Gabriel carrying either a scepter or a spray of olive. Later, artists changed the olive to a spray of Madonna lilies.

Parsley was known as one of the sacred funeral plants to the ancient Greeks and Romans. It was placed on graves and served at funeral banquets. Later, the plant was consecrated to St. Peter in his role as heavenly gatekeeper. Good Friday was considered a day of mourning for European Christians and little household activity was conducted. It was, however, the day to plant parsley after returning from church. The slow germination of this plant, according to legend, was due to the necessity for the seed to descend to hell at least three times before it sprouted. Others said it had to go to the Devil and back nine times, and since the Devil liked it as well as everyone else, he kept a little each time, and that is why it appeared so spottily when it did finally come up.

Passion flower — This plant was so-named because of the supposed resemblance of the finely cut corona in the center of the blossoms to the Crown of Thorns and of the other parts of the flower to the instruments of the Passion of Our Lord.

Potatoes — The Spaniards discovered potatoes in the Peruvian Andes in the early part of the sixteenth century. One of Pizarro's priests is credited with bringing the potato to Spain, even though Columbus is sometimes mentioned. (It was the sweet potato and not the white one which Columbus found in the West Indies.) Most Europeans at first thought them to be poisonous and were very slow to accept them as a food item. Many people also shunned them because they were not mentioned in the Bible. In particular, the Scots refused to eat them as late as 1728. The Irish found a way around this by planting them on Good Friday and sprinkling the soil liberally with holy water. Potatoes became lifesavers during the famines in France in the late eighteenth and early nineteenth centuries. Parmentier, a great friend of the court, wanted to encourage the peasants to use potatoes. To that end, Marie Antoinette wore potato blossoms in her hair and King Louis XVI wore one on his lapel. The fields outside Paris were planted with potatoes and then heavily guarded so as to show that something valuable was growing there. The ruse worked, and the peasants raided the fields.

Poinsettia — A charming Mexican legend tells that a poor little boy went to church on Christmas Eve, sad because he had no gift for the Holy Child. He knelt outside the church and prayed fervently, telling the Christ Child that he dared not approach with empty hands. When he stood, at his feet he saw a beautiful green plant with dazzling red blooms, as if in answer to his prayers. Taking the beautiful flowers, he joyously entered the church with his gift.

Redbud — Because of its attractive flowers, many persons know the redbud as a cultivated shrub or small tree over most of temperate North America. It is sometimes called the Judas tree. This name comes from the legend that it was on a near eastern tree of this type that Judas hanged himself, and that its flowers at the time were white but turned color with shame and have blushed ever since.

Rest harrow (wild licorice) — One tradition says that this was the plant from which the crown of thorns was plaited.

Roses, along with lilies, are the two most representative flowers of the Virgin Mary, and legends concerning them abound. One old legend relates that St. Thomas, not believing the reports about the assumption of the Virgin, had her tomb opened. Inside, instead of her body, he found the tomb to be filled with lilies and roses. Roses today are also associated with St. Thérèse of Lisieux, the Little Flower, because of her promise to send a "shower of roses" from heaven.

Rosemary is one of the best-loved herbs worldwide and is a symbol of love and fidelity, often having been worn at weddings. St. Thomas More wrote that he let this herb run wild all over his garden because his bees loved it, and also because it was a flower of memory and friendship. He also pointed out that it was the chosen emblem of English funeral wakes and burial grounds. In France, it was carried by mourners at funerals and thrown into the open grave on the coffin. The Spaniards revere the plant as one of the bushes that gave shelter to the Virgin Mary on the flight to Egypt, and both in Spain and Italy it was considered a safeguard against witches and evil spirits. It is also said that the Virgin dried her cloak on the plant, imparting the color of the sky to the flowers. One old legend compares the growth of the rosemary with the height of the Savior, and declares that after 33 years the plant may increase in breadth but will not increase in height. The traditional European Easter meal is still lamb, flavored with the fragrant herb.

The plant's association with Mary gave it a role as protector against evil. It was used as a charm against the evil eye and was laid in cradles to protect children from nightmares. It was burned in churches as incense, and some said rosemary would refuse to grow in the gardens of the wicked, which must have given anxious moments to some pious homeowners. Hungarian queen's water, a miraculous liquid for the cure of many illnesses including arthritis of the hands and legs, was popular for many years. Attributed to St. Elizabeth, Queen of Hungary, the recipe called for three parts of distilled brandy and two parts of the leaf and flower of rosemary.

Rue (herb of grace) — At one time in England, the holy water was sprinkled from bushes made of rue at the ceremony usually preceding the Sunday Mass, for which reason the plant was often called the herb of repentance or herb of grace.

Sage was considered a cure for teething babies in the Middle Ages. The babies wore twelve leaves of sage, denoting the twelve apostles.

Wood sorrell (*Oxalis acetosella*) — This plant, called "alleluia" because it springs forth during the time of year when the alleluia was sung in churches, is considered by many to be the plant used by St. Patrick to demonstrate the Trinity to the ancient Irish, although a tiny kind of clover is sometimes accepted as the true shamrock. Fra Angelico often depicted this plant in his paintings.

Southernwood (*Artemisia abrotanum*) — It was the habit to include a spray of this plant in country bouquets presented to lovers, and St. Francis de Sales said, "To love in the midst of sweets, little children could do that, but to love in the bitterness of Wormwood is a sure sign of our affectionate fidelity." It used to be the custom for women to carry large bunches of this plant and balm into church so that their keen scent would prevent people from feeling drowsy.

Spearmint — Our common spearmint is another herb that was dedicated to the Virgin and was often called *Erba Santa Maria* or *Menthe de Notre Dame*. It was used as a strewing herb on the floor of churches, and to repel mice.

Mint was one of the herbs grown in Britain by the Romans, but with the decay of the Empire it fell out of use for a time. The Crusaders discovered it again and brought it home to Europe, where it found a multitude of uses. Today's mint-flavored toothpaste is not something new — it was used in Europe several hundred years ago to rub on teeth to whiten and brighten them.

Star of Bethlehem (*ornithogalum arabicum*) is supposed to have first appeared on the earth on the night of Christ's birth. According to the legend, the star that led the three wise men to the Child burst into thousands of fragments after stopping at its destination, and each fragment that touched the earth turned into a flower.

Strawberry — The strawberry was early dedicated to the Virgin Mary. An old superstition tells that if a mother came to heaven's gates with the stain of strawberries on her lips, she was cast down to hell for trespassing in the Virgin's fields. In parts of Europe, the Virgin was said to accompany children when they picked strawberries on St. John's Day, and on that day no mother who has lost a child will eat a strawberry lest her little one get none in Paradise.

Tansy was one of the strewing herbs used in churches and another of the plants dedicated to the Virgin. It is connected with some interesting old Easter customs. Archbishops, bishops, and priests played handball with men of their congregation, and a tansy cake was the reward of the victors. These cakes, made from the young leaves of the plant mixed with eggs, were throught to purify the body after the strict diet of Lent. Later, the cakes were eaten on Easter Day as a remembrance of the bitter herbs eaten by the Jews at Passover.

Tarragon was used to prevent fatigue. In the Middle Ages, many pilgrims tucked leaves of this herb into their shoes to sustain them on their long, foot-wearying journey to the Holy Land.

Milk thistle — There is a tradition that the milk-white veins of the leaves of this plant originated in the milk of the Virgin which once fell upon a plant of the thistle. Hence it was called Our Lady's thistle, and the Latin name has the same derivation. The Carline thistle is so named because when a horrible pestilence broke out in the army of Charlemagne, he prayed earnestly and in his sleep an angel appeared who shot an arrow from a crossbow, telling the pious emperor to mark the plant on which it fell, for with that plant he might cure his army of the pestilence. The herb so miraculously indicated was the thistle, which does appear to have medicinal qualities very like those of elecampane, and it can be used as an antiseptic.

Thyme, by ancient tradition, was one of the herbs that formed the bed of the Virgin. It became associated with death, and is one of the fragrant flowers planted on graves in Wales. The Order of Oddfellows carried sprigs of thyme at funerals and threw them into the grave of a dead brother. The knights riding off to the Crusades often carried scarves embroidered by their wives and sweethearts which showed a bee hovering over a sprig of thyme, a symbol of courage and energy.

Tobacco, first introduced to England in 1586 by Sir Walter Raleigh, met with violent opposition, including a Papal Bull.

Vervain (*Verbena officinalis*) was also known as the herb of grace. Although the name "verbena" was the classical name for altar plants in general, and the druids included it in their lustral water, there was a legend that it was discovered on the Mount of Calvary where it staunched the wounds of the crucified Savior. It was crossed and blessed with a commemorative verse when gathered and worn around the neck to fend off headaches and snakes, and for general good luck and good eyesight.

Winter cress, a close relative of watercress, has as part of its botanical name "*Barbarea*," because in some parts of Europe it is the only green plant that can be picked on St. Barbara's Day, December 4.

Gardening Customs From Around the World

There are hundreds of Catholic customs worldwide that in some way involve gardens, harvests, flowers, and other gifts from nature. From the golden rose of the Pope to the humble shamrock worn by Irishmen everywhere on St. Patrick's day, the plant kingdom has enriched Catholic life through the centuries. Only a few of these customs are mentioned here.

Beating the Bounds — England

An old village custom dates back to the days in England when the tilled fields of the parish were blessed at Rogationtide.[†] The time-honored custom was for the pastor and people of the village to circumambulate the parish, and came to be known as the "beating of the bounds." A statue of Our Lady was generally carried in the colorful processions, which formed a liturgy-on-the-move with prayer stops at each of the cardinal points of the compass.

Harvest Festival — Poland

In Poland, when the harvests were gathered, the people of the fields gave thanks and celebrated an age-old custom called *"Dozynki."* On a warm Sunday in late August, the tillers of the soil with their whole families walked gaily to the manor house to the sound of traditional tunes. The young girls, in colorful native costumes, headed the procession carrying large wreaths made of the harvested rye or wheat, intertwined with poppies and bachelor buttons. The fruit of the orchard —plums, pears, and apples— was tied to the wreaths with yellow, red, blue, and purple ribbons. At the manor house, the landlord invited the people in for a large feast and singing, dancing, and games for the children completed the festive celebration. The feast commemorates the joy and gratitude for fair weather, good crops, and the bounty of God's nature to mankind.

The Didukh — Ukraine

The didukh is a sheaf of grain made from the best wheat or grain of the field. It is decorated with flowers, ribbons, a small wreath of sweet basil and other herbs, or an embroidered towel. At Christmas, the didukh is carried into the home amid traditional greetings of "Christ is born!" Thanks are expressed to God for the good health and fortune of the family. In pre-Christian Kiev, when the sun god was worshiped and the winter celebrations commemorated the family ancestors, the didukh, or forefather, was a symbol of the deceased members of the family. The people believed that the souls of good people looked over the fields in the summer and protected the harvest from all sorts of natural disasters. In the winter, the souls came into the home when the didukh was carried into the house. This pagan symbolism was changed into a Christian one, and the didukh now symbolizes the Christian belief in an after-life, as well as a being a symbol of a bountiful harvest. At the end of the holiday season, the didukh was carried out of the home and either burned or scattered over the fields or in the orchard.

The Advent Wreath — Germany

The Advent Wreath originated a few hundred years ago among the Lutherans of eastern Germany. It probably was suggested by one of the many light symbols used in folklore at the end of November and beginning of December. At that time, our pre-Christian forefathers began to celebrate the month of Yule with the burning of lights and fires. The medieval Christians kept many light and fire symbols alive as popular traditions, and in the sixteenth century the custom started of using such lights as a religious symbol of Advent. The practice quickly spread among the Protestants of eastern Germany and was soon accepted by Protestants and Catholics in other parts of the country. Today, its use has spread worldwide.

The wreath is a wreath of evergreens made in various sizes, with four candles representing the four weeks of Advent. Daily the family gathers for a short religious exercise. Each Sunday another candle is lit until all four candles announce the approaching birthday of the Lord.

The Christmas Tree — Germany

The use of Christmas trees is a fairly recent custom in all countries outside of Germany, and even there it gained its popularity as recently as the end of the last century. The tree has its origin in a combination of two medieval religious symbols, the Paradise tree and the Christmas light or candle.

About the eleventh century, religious plays were performed in or near churches. One of the most popular of the "mystery plays" was the Paradise play, which told the story of creation and the expulsion of Adam and Eve from Paradise after their sin. The play ended with a consoling promise of a coming Savior, and was most popular at Advent. A fir tree hung with apples represented the Garden of Eden and was the only prop on stage. The mystery plays were gradually forbidden in the fifteenth century because of abuses, but the people were so attached to the Paradise tree that they began putting it up in their homes in honor of the feast day of Adam and Eve on December 24. Although the Latin Church never officially celebrated Adam and Eve as saints, the Eastern Churches do and their feast spread into Europe. The Paradise tree stood for the tree of life as well as the tree of sin; in addition to the apples representing the fruit of sin, the tree bore wafers representing the Holy Eucharist, the fruit of life. Later the wafers were replaced by candy and pastry representing the sweet fruit of Christ's redemption.

In western Germany during the sixteenth century, the people began to transfer the decorations from the Christmas pyramid, a form of candle holder, to the tree. Thus, glass balls, tinsel, and stars were added. During the seventeenth century the lights were added.

The Christmas tree arrived in America with the first wave of German immigrants about 1700. Its popularity today extends throughout the world.

St. Barbara's Cherry — Slovakia

It was customary among the Czechs and Slovaks, and also in Austria and some sections of central Europe, to break a branch off a cherry or peach tree on St. Barbara's Day, December 4, place it in a pot of water in the kitchen, and keep it in warm air. The twig would then burst into blossom at Christmas to make a festive decoration. These branches were considered omens of good luck. The girl who tended the branch would find a good husband within a year if she succeeded in getting it to bloom exactly on Christmas Eve. In Ukraine, the same custom was kept in honor of St. Catherine. The young girls would cut the branch on the morning of St. Catherine's Day, and if it sprouted before Malanka (New Year's Eve), she would have good luck in the new year.

St. Stephen's Horses — Central Europe

Although there is no historical basis for his association with horses, St. Stephen the martyr has been venerated as the patron of horses. It was a general practice among the farmers in central Europe to decorate their horses on Stephen's Day and bring them to church to be blessed by the priest. Afterwards, the horse was ridden three times around the church. Horse food, mostly hay and oats, was blessed on this day, December 26, and the people threw kernels of these blessed oats at one another and at their domestic animals. Water and salt were often blessed on this day and kept to be fed to the horses in case of sickness. The women baked special breads in the form of horseshoes to be eaten on the feast.

Feast of the Seven Sorrows — Spain and South America

In the Latin countries, especially in Spain and South America, the Feast of the Seven Sorrows is a great day of popular devotion. The people thronged the churches to visit the shrine of the Sorrowful Mother. This shrine is radiant with many lights and is richly decorated with flowers, palms, and with shade-grown clusters of pale young wheat. In central Europe, the feast is called *Schmerzenfreitag*, or Friday of Sorrows, and after the popular devotions in the churches a soup consisting of seven bitter herbs is served in the homes for supper.

Blessing of Palms — Italy

As soon as the Church obtained her freedom in the fourth century, the faithful in Jerusalem began to re-enact the solemn entry of Christ into the city on the Sunday before Easter, holding a procession in which they carried branches and sang the "Hosanna." In the early Latin Church on this day, the people held aloft twigs of olives. The rite of the solemn blessing of "palms" seems to have originated in the Frankish kingdom about the beginning of the eighth century. The custom gained great momentum throughout Europe in the medieval times with a procession of clergy and laity carrying palms to a designated spot, where the palms were blessed. Our Lord was represented in the procession either by the Blessed Sacrament or by a wooden statue of Christ sitting on a donkey, which was pulled on a wheeled platform. These *Palmesel*, or palm donkeys, are still seen in some museums of European cities. A similar figure was later carried to the New World by the Spanish and in our own times was used in the rites of the *Penitentes* of the American Southwest.

In France and England, the procession included a trip to the cemetery, where the graves were decorated and visited on Palm Sunday. Since true palms were unobtainable in many countries of Europe, various plants were used and became known as "palms," including the yew in Ireland and pussy willows in England and Germany. Centuries ago it was the custom to bless not only branches, but flowers as well, and the custom has been retained in some parts of Europe. The name of the day in some countries reflects this and it is often known as Flower Sunday. In many countries, "palm bouquets" are made with flowers intertwined with the "palms," and affixed to a stick or rod. In the Latin countries and the United States, palm leaves are often shaped into little crosses to be kept in the homes throughout the year. In Austria, Bavaria, and the Slavic countries, the farmers and their families walked through the fields praying and singing hymns on the afternoon of Palm Sunday. They placed a spring of blessed palm in each lot or pasture and in every barn and stable to avert bad weather and disease and to draw God's blessing on the year's harvest.

Grottoes of St. James — England

The body of St. James the Apostle, martyred for the Faith in Jerusalem, was later taken to Spain and buried in Compostela, where his shrine became a great center of pilgrimage. The symbol of a successful pilgrimage became a cockle shell, and returning pilgrims wore one on their coat or hat. During the Middle Ages, many pilgrims went to Compostela from England. To raise money to help the poorer pilgrims, it became a tradition to build small grottoes of scallop shells. People would pay a penny, light a candle in the grotto, and say a prayer for the pilgrim. Later, English children took over the custom, and as late as the Second World War these small grottoes in honor of St. James were made, especially near the coast.

Pentecost Dew — Northern Europe

In rural sections of northern Europe, pious superstition ascribes a special power of healing to the dew that falls during Pentecost night. The people walk barefoot through the grass on the early morning of the feast. With pieces of bread, they collect the dew and feed it to their domestic animals as a protection against disease and accidents.

The Pentecost Tree — Russia

About the middle of the eighteenth century, a group of German Catholics settled on the farming region around the Volga River. After about a hundred years in the area, many of their descendents began a general migration to the United States and settled in the farming region of Kansas. One custom they brought with them, but which is no longer in vogue, was the Pentecost tree. On the Saturday before Pentecost, or on Pentecost, the young men of the villages planted a tree in front of the homes of girls they liked. It was considered an honor to have a *Pfingstbaum*, or Pentecost tree, planted in front of your home.

Day of Wreaths — France and Central Europe

In France and many sections of central Europe, the feast of Corpus Christi was known as the Day of Wreaths. Huge bouquets of flowers were borne on the top of wooden poles, and wreaths and bouquets of exquisite flowers in various colors were attached to flags and banners, houses, and green arches that spanned the streets. The men wore small wreaths on their left arms in the processions and the girls worn them on their heads. The monstrance containing the Blessed Sacrament was adorned with a wreath of choice flowers. In Poland, the wreaths were blessed on the eve of the feast. After the feast, the people decorated their homes with them. These wreaths were hung on the walls, windows, and doors of the houses and were put up on poles in gardens, fields, and pastures with a prayer for protection and blessing upon the growing harvest.

Harvest Festivals — Worldwide

From pre-Christian times, thanksgiving celebrations took place at the conclusion of a successful harvest. These celebrations were Christianized during the Middle Ages and even today in many rural sections of the world pious customs and superstitions attend the ending of the harvest. In southern France, the last sheaf of the harvest was tied in the form of a cross, decorated with ribbons and flowers, and after the celebration was placed in the house to be kept as a token of blessing and good fortune. In Hungary, the Feast of the Assumption included great thanksgiving solemnities for the grain harvest, and the people came from all parts of the country to Budapest, carrying the best samples of their produce. In Poland, harvest wreaths were brought to Warsaw. The wreaths were made of the straw of the last sheaf, beautifully decorated with flowers, fruits, nuts, and ribbons, and blessed in churches by the priests. From medieval times, the most common thanksgiving celebrations were held on the feast of St. Martin of Tours

(Martinmas) on November 11. It was a holiday in Germany and several countries of central Europe. The meal was a traditional roast goose and St. Martin's wine, the first lot made from the grapes of the recent harvest, was the drink of choice. Children in Germany made St. Martin's lamps. During World War II, due to a lack of other supplies, the children carved their lamps from turnips and sugar beets. Martinmas is still a popular feast in many parts of Germany. Although some home crafters will make their lamps, most purchase inexpensive St. Martin's lamps at the store.

Assumption Blessing of Herbs and Fruits — Worldwide

August 15, the Feast of the Assumption, has called forth special blessings since medieval times. In central Europe the feast itself was called "Our Lady's Herb Day," and in the Alpine provinces the blessing of herbs is still bestowed before the solemn service of the Assumption.

The Eastern rites have similar blessings. The Syrians used to celebrate a special feast of "Our Lady of Herbs" on May 15. The Armenian faithful bring the first grapes from the vineyards to church on Assumption Day and have them solemnly blessed by the priests. The family eats them before tasting the rest of the new harvest.

In Sicily, the people fasted from fruit during the first two weeks of August in honor of the Blessed Virgin, and on the feast itself had fruit blessed in church which they ate for dinner. They then presented one another with baskets of fruit. In all the European Christian countries before the Reformation, the priest used to ride through the pastures on Assumption Day blessing the farms, orchards, fields, and gardens. In the Alpine regions of France, the animals were gathered around a large cross decorated with branches and flowers and blessed by the priest, who sprinkled them with holy water. Beginning in the Middle Ages in the German-speaking sections of Europe, the days from August 15 to September 15 were called Our Lady's Thirty Days, and even today Assumption shrines sometimes show Mary clad in a robe covered with ears of grain.

Annunciation Bread — Russia

In Russia, priests would bless large wafers of wheat flour and give them to the faithful. At home, the father would hand a small piece of the wafer to each member of the family and to the servants, who received it with a bow and ate it in silence. Later on they would take the crumbs of the Annunciation bread out into the fields and, with pious superstition, bury them in the ground as a protection against blight, hail, frost, and drought. In central Europe the farmers put a picture of the Assumption in the seed grain while asking Our Lady's help for the crop.

Our Lady of the Grape Harvest — France

In the wine-growing sections of France, the Nativity of Mary, September 8, is the day of the grape-harvest festival. The owners of the vineyards bring their choicest fruits to church to be blessed, and afterward tie some of them to the hands of the statue of the Virgin.

The Wearing of the Green — Ireland

Although the custom of wearing green on St. Patrick's Day did not begin until over a thousand years after his death, the charming practice of displaying the shamrock is traced to the legend that St. Patrick taught King Oengus the doctrine of the Holy Trinity by using the shamrock as an illustration. Patrick's Day heralded the beginning of spring in Ireland, and it is still regarded as the best time in many sections of the country for the farmers to begin sowing and planting potatoes.

St. Brigid's Cross — Ireland

In rural Ireland, a couple just taking possession of a farm or homestead would nail a St. Brigid's cross under the barn eaves. The cross is made from rushes, straw, or wood. In some areas, it is placed in dwellings and on farm buildings on the eve of the feast of St. Brigid, February 1. The legend of the cross is that Brigid, renowned for her charity, once acted as nurse to a pagan chieftain. While he slept, she made a cross with some rushes from the floor. On waking, the chieftain asked why she formed the cross. Our saint told him the story of Calvary. He was deeply impressed, and his subsequent conversion and return to health were attributed to her prayers.

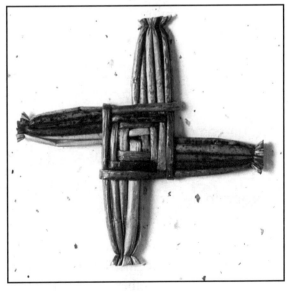

St. Brigid's Cross

St. Joseph's Day — Italy

In some parts of Italy and in central Europe, St. Joseph's Day is celebrated by the farmers as the beginning of spring. They light candles in honor of the saint, put little shrines with his picture in their gardens and orchards, and have their fields blessed by the priest. In Sicily and the United States whereever Sicilian immigrants settled, the custom of St. Joseph's table is popular. A large altar is prepared in the saint's honor, covered with many traditional food items. A meal is served and food and donations are given to the poor. In the United States the custom varies slightly depending on the region, but everywhere it is a happy, joyful celebration honoring this saint of the people and our less fortunate brothers.

Well-Dressing — England

The tradition of well-dressing at Ascensiontide dates back to the Black Death, when the people at Tissington were spared and attributed their good fortune to the purity of the water supply. During the drought of 1615, many rivers and lakes dried up, and the people of the area came to Tissington, where the faithful wells continued to give water. Here, and at a number of other famous wells in Derbyshire, it was a custom to make boarded frames covered with damp soil to place over the wells.

A variety of beautiful designs, all with religious themes, are created from flowers, berries, and leaves. A short service is held at each well and it is solemnly blessed.

Weave St. Brigid's Cross

Supplies needed

16 pieces of straw or other weaving material, each 8" long

thread to tie off ends

Although the *crosóg Brigde* (St. Brigid's Cross) is usually made from rushes or straw in Ireland, you can easily weave one of the decorative crosses from many materials. Any limber material, such as a vine or long grass, will do. If you have access to stalks of wheat, the cross takes on an even deeper dimension if you leave the head of grain which, when woven, will form the ends of the cross's arms.

Fold the first 2 pieces in half, slipping 1 side of 1 piece through the fold of the other. Fold a third piece in half over the second piece. (See the diagram.) Continue adding folded pieces, lapping each piece over the one

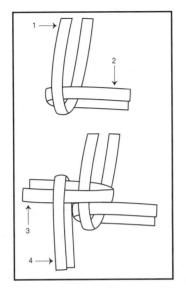

St. Brigid's cross assembly

you just placed previously. When all 16 pieces have been placed, take the loose ends of the last piece and tuck them under the piece they face. Pinch the loose ends of each arm of the cross together and tie tightly with twine. Clip the loose ends as close as possible to the tie.

Make a Didukh

Since we live in a city, we can't bring in a first sheaf of wheat or any other grain. But we can certainly celebrate the birth of Christ, and we made a lovely wall hanging in His honor in the traditional way.

Directions

Punch a hole in the small piece of heavy paper. Make your hole about ½" from the short side. This will be your hanger. Draw a line about ½" from the bottom of the hole, across the card. This is the line that will mark the top of where you will use your glue. Do not put any glue above this line.

Draw a thin line of hot glue from the center of your glue line straight down to the bottom of the card. Glue on 1 piece of wheat, making certain that the grain of the wheat is above the glue line. To avoid burning your fingers, use the eraser end of a pencil to press the wheat straw into the hot glue.

On the left of the first line of glue, draw a thin bead or line of glue from the glue line down to the bottom of the card, and attach a piece of wheat with the head of the wheat above the glue line. If your grain points slightly left, this will be fine. Repeat on the right side. Continue placing pieces of wheat until you have covered the card. This will probably take about 9 pieces of wheat.

Begin again at the middle and glue on another 5 to 7 pieces of wheat. This

Supplies needed

piece of card stock or heavy paper, 1"x4"

hole punch

dried wheat

hot-glue gun

ribbon

will form a second layer and make your didukh seem more three-dimensional.

When the entire card is covered by the stems of the wheat, cut the bottom portion of the wheat off. The stem part should be about 1½ the length of the top.

Glue a piece of ribbon onto the back of the didukh. Cross it over on the front side and attach with a piece of glue. Glue on a decoration. We used a piece of glass rock from the aquarium and fabric paint. You can use dried flowers or other small decorations.

This is an inexpensive gift to present to your neighbors on Christmas day with the traditional greeting of "Christ is Born."

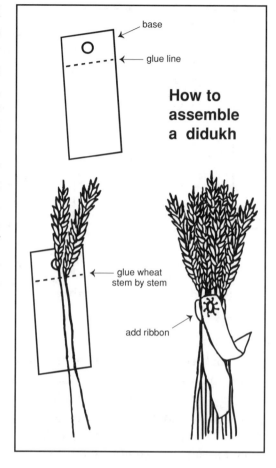

base

glue line

How to assemble a didukh

glue wheat stem by stem

add ribbon

Make St. James's Grotto

You can make a simple St. James's Grotto to decorate a summer table and remind you of the custom adapted by the English children.

This is an outside project; plaster in your water pipes calls for a plumber!

Supplies needed

plaster of paris

seashells

small candle in glass container

old margarine tub or other disposable plastic container

In a throw-away container, mix enough plaster (or cement) according to package directions to pour about 2" high in the bottom of your plastic tub. The plaster should be about the texture of a thick cake-mix.

Center the glass candle in the container, allowing it to sink down slightly in the plaster.

Arrange a few seashells decoratively around the candle. If your plaster is too thin, the shells will sink in too far. In this case, pull them out and rinse them off. Jiggle the plaster to smooth the top and wait about 15 minutes before trying to place the shells again.

When the shells are arranged, let the entire project dry completely for several hours before carefully unmolding it. Display your candle on an outside table; arrange other shells around it if you like.

St. James's Grotto

Endnote

† Rogation days were special days of penitential prayer. Two sets of rogation days were kept from early Christian times: The major rogation on April 25, and the minor rogations on the Monday, Tuesday, and Wednesday before Ascension Thursday. In 1969, the rogation days were replaced by periods of prayer for the needs of the people, and the observance of these periods may take place at different times of the year depending on the decision of the conferences of local bishops.

Sacred Gardens

The Vatican Gardens

The territory on the right bank of the Tiber between Monte Mario and Gianicolo was known in antiquity as the *Ager Vaticanus*. The origin of the name is uncertain, but it is possible that it comes from a vanished Etruscan town called Vaticum. The district did not belong to ancient Rome, nor was it included within the city walls built by Emperor Aurelian. In the imperial gardens situated in this section was the Circus of Nero. At the foot of the Vatican Hill lay the ancient Basilica of St. Peter. By extensive purchases of land, the medieval popes acquired possession of the whole hill. Between 848 and 852, Leo IV surrounded the whole settlement with a wall. Today, the Vatican, which is the locus for the activities of the Holy See, is located within the Vatican City State, the last remnant of the Papal States.

The Vatican has served as the chief residence of the Pope since the end of the Avignon captivity in 1377. (From 1307 to 1377 and for seven papacies, the Holy See operated from the extraterritorial papal city of Avignon, France, instead of Rome.)

The Vatican Gardens comprise a third of the Vatican territory. They are made up of lawns and woods, crisscrossed with avenues and adorned by artificial caves, kiosks, monumental statues, and fountains. Through the centuries, various popes and groups from many nations have enriched the beauty of the gardens with donations of statuary, fountains, buildings, and plants. The beautiful gardens provide a place where the Pope can walk and reflect in the open air.

For Catholics, the Pope is considered the successor of St. Peter, and near the center of the Vatican grounds, in the midst of a palm grove, is a bronze statue of the saint. It was once part of the monument erected in the Court of the *"Pigna"* to commemorate the First Vatican Council (1869-1870). Another statue of St. Peter, this one titled "St. Peter in Chains," can be seen through the trees of the English garden. Sculpted in 1887 by Amalia Dupré, the first woman artist represented in the Vatican, it alludes to the years of virtual captivity of the Pope during the occupation of Rome by the new Italian state at the turn of the century. Like most of the statues in the garden, it is dedicated to Leo XIII.

In the English garden, the vegetation is allowed to grow naturally. In a clearing along the upper border of this garden is the little chapel of the "*Madonna della Guardia*," with a reproduction of the statue which overlooks the entry to the port of Genoa. This statue was donated by the Genovese to their fellow citizen, Pope Benedict XV. At the lower end of the English garden is a Chinese pavilion, donated by Chinese Catholics to Pius XI in 1933 to commemorate the nineteenth centenary of the death of Christ. This pavilion was a favorite resting place of Pope John XXIII.

In another area of the gardens, near the boundary of the Vatican territory, is the Square of the Madonna of Lourdes. Here there is a cement reproduction of the Grotto of Lourdes (Massabielle), where the Madonna appeared before St. Bernadette Soubirous in 1858. The grotto was donated to Pope Leo XIII by the Bishop of Tarbes, the diocese which includes the city of Lourdes. Images of the donor and the Pope are represented in mosaic above the grotto. The original altar of the Lourdes grotto, donated to Pope John XXIII, is still used on special occasions.

Passing through one of the most attractive and shady areas of the gardens, with little fountains and benches decorated with ancient marble, the visitor descends to the seventeenth-century Fountain of the Eagle by the Dutch artist Jan van Santen. As with all the fountains in the Vatican, the water comes from the Lake of Bracciano, abut 40 kilometers from Rome. The eagle and the griffin are the symbols of the Borghese family of Pope Paul V (1605-1621), who commissioned the fountain.

Another fountain is known as the Fountain of the Mirrors, and was probably built for Paul V at the beginning of the seventeenth century. It is an elegant *aedicula* with side entrances and two small fountains, one inside and one outside, splendidly decorated with blue and gold mosaic. They are inspired by the fountains of Pompeii.

A third fountain of note is the monumental Fountain of the Sacrament, so-called because its jets of water resemble a monstrance surrounded by six candles. Also the work of van Santen, this fountain is built on the site of an ancient entrance to the Vatican.

Near the statue of St. Peter stands a small turreted building called the House of the Gardener because of its present use. This building was probably one of the buildings erected inside the Leonine walls by Pope Innocent III (1198-1216).

An Italian garden contains shrubs and flower-beds, symmetrically trimmed and arranged in a formal manner. A rose garden contains beautiful flowers. In other areas, vineries have been laid out and vegetables are cultivated. In one part, wild flowers grow in an oak grove. Formerly, the Vatican gardens even contained a number of exotic animals, ranging from lions to ostriches.

Traditionally, the popes have found in the beauty of their gardens a place of rest, solitude, and reflection. The Vatican gardens are a place to pray and contemplate the wonders of the Creator. By enhancing the beauty of our own gardens, we, too, can create a place of contemplation and better appreciate our Creator.

Everlastings

Since mankind began to live in houses, he has tried to bring nature indoors to decorate his living space. The passion for fancy floral and nature decorations had its heyday in the Victorian age, and today's crafters are rediscovering the fun of preserving nature and using it for decorations.

Everlasting Shell Bouquet

The Victorians often combined seashells with what they called "everlastings." These were flowers and leaves carefully dried for preservation. My Aunt Ora spent hours carefully drying flowers that she later crafted into many different types of arrangements and gifts. Today's scientists have come up with an even easier way to dry flowers that helps them retain much of their natural color when dried.

At most craft stores, you can purchase microwavable flower-drying crystals. These are silica gel crystals, a dessicant. In minutes you can now dry flowers for "everlastings" in your kitchen microwave.

You will need about two pounds of silica gel. This can be reused over and over again. You will also need a heavy plastic microwavable container at least three inches deep, and a scoop. The type of spatula or scoop used for deep fat frying will be helpful when retrieving your flowers from the drying medium.

Put about an inch of the crystals into the container. Arrange your flowers face up so they are not touching and carefully scoop crystals over them until they are completely covered. Put the container in the microwave for one to three minutes on high. Allow to cool completely before carefully scooping the flowers out. Gently shake, blow on, or use a soft brush to remove silica gel that remains on the flowers.

Dried flowers are quite fragile and brittle, so you will have to be gentle when working with them. Some, such as rosebuds, are sturdier. It is this fragile beauty, however, that is one of the attractions.

Some flowers dry better than others. Roses and rosebuds, azaleas, Johnny-jump-ups, and many darker-colored flowers seem to do best. White flowers often turn an unattractive shade. A variety of small ferns and leaves keep their color well when dried. Experiment with whatever you have growing in your yard.

Make An Everlasting Shell Bouquet

Begin by slipping the ribbon through the ring, centering it so that an equal amount of ribbon falls from either side of the ring.

Glue the 2 pieces of ribbon together with a small dab of hot glue about 1½" down from the ring. Make 2 thin lines of glue about ½" apart on the back of the shell from the top to the bottom.

Press the ribbon hanger onto the glue, using the eraser end of a pencil to avoid burning your finger. The piece with the ring should extend about 2" above your shell.

Allow to dry. Hold your project up by the ring to make certain the shell is thoroughly glued to the ribbon. If not, reinforce with more glue at the top of the project.

Using your hot-glue gun, glue a small bouquet in the center of the shell. Begin by putting a long, spikey leaf or two pointing down. Make one spikey leaf going up. Then glue in your everlasting flowers in colors to match your ribbon.

Supplies needed

1 large flat seashell *

18" piece of 1½"-wide ribbon

1 plastic curtain-rod ring

hot-glue gun

scissors

everlasting dried flowers and leaves

clear acrylic spray — optional

clear glitter — optional

When you are satisfied with your bouquet, spray a very light coat of clear acrylic spray on the flowers. This will bring out their colors and help to make them sturdier. If you like, shake on a tiny bit of clear glitter for a fancier effect.

*If you cannot find a shell, cut a circle or diamond shape of gold or silver paper from the back of an old greeting card to use as a base for your everlastings.

Fill a Shoe Vase

Supplies needed

child's shoe

florist foam

3 or 5 artificial flowers

dried greenery

knife

I needed a tiny bit of color for a vacant spot on the bookshelf. I spied one of Maxie's outgrown shoes that had lost its mate. So I cut a piece of florist foam and added 3 artificial flowers and some greenery. What a nice gift that would make for a doting grandmother!

If the shoe is pretty worn, you can paint it with gold or silver spray paint if you like. Laces could be replaced with ribbon or braid. Cut a piece of floral foam to put inside the shoe to hold the arrangement. Stick in short pieces of dried greenery and 3 or 5 silk flowers.

Gardens to Share

A number of church, school, and civic groups throughout the country have come up with a community effort to reinforce the Gospel values of loving your neighbor and feeding the poor. The groups donate their time and effort to farm vegetable gardens. The produce grown is then donated to the poor. Even in the largest cities, the use of a small plot of land is often available for the asking.

For the past seven years, the members of Cana, a small faith community in Colchester, Conneticut, have worked a large garden plot together

Shoe Vase

from May through October. The vegetables are grown for, delivered to, and sometimes even cooked for the poor of the Diocese of Norwich at St. Vincent de Paul soup kitchens in Middletown and Norwich. Their gifts go far in feeding the 150 daily patrons.

Readers of this book who enjoy gardening are encouraged to get a group together to grow a garden for the poor. A suitable organization to distribute the bounty of your harvest can be located through your diocese, if you don't already have one in mind.

Mr. Potato

Long before the clever plastic potato-head toys were invented, we made little people out of potatoes and other vegetables. It was an inexpensive and easy craft for kids. We took that idea and combined it with the more modern chia pet idea to find a way that today's kids can also have a fun afternoon making Mr. Potato, and then watching his hair grow.

Buy a little rye-grass seed from your garden supply store or a little chia seed from the health-food store and keep it on hand for a rainy day.

Draw around our pattern on page 96 and use scissors to cut the feet and ears from the bottom of a plastic foam meat tray.

Cut a small bit of the top of the potato off, leaving a flat surface. With a spoon, hollow out a hole in the top of the potato about 1" deep and to within about ¼" of the edge of the potato.

Paint 2 round, white circles with the white-out or acrylic paint for the eyes. Paint a white area for the inside of the mouth to simulate the teeth. Use pins to add 2 small beads or buttons for the inside part of the eyes. Pin on a button nose. Outline the outside of the teeth with white glue and glue on red yarn to form lips. Cut a small slit on either side of the potato to add the ears. Using 2 nails about an inch or more in length, attach the feet to the base of Mr. Potato.

Supplies needed

rye-grass seed or chia seed

potato

white-out or white acrylic paint

meat tray

button

small piece of red yarn

straight pins

2 small colored beads or buttons

soil

knife

spoon

scissors

white glue

2 nails with heads

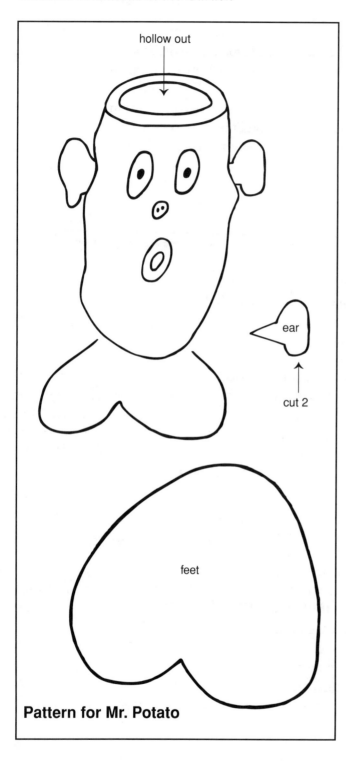

hollow out

ear

cut 2

feet

Pattern for Mr. Potato

More adventuresome children can use other found objects to form the facial features. For example, they may want to pin on paper eyelashes or craft glasses from a paper clip. A scrap of red felt makes a great tongue. Their imagination will make their Mr. Potato unique.

When the potato is decorated, carefully fill the hole in the top with soil. Sprinkle about a half-teaspoon of rye-grass seed or chia seed over the dirt and dampen the dirt thoroughly.

Stand Mr. Potato in a sunny windowsill while you wait for his hair to grow. The potato will help to keep the soil moist, but you may need to sprinkle a little water on the top of his head daily. Rye grass will sprout in 5 to 6 days. If his hair gets too unruly, the children will enjoy giving him a haircut with nail scissors!

Ecologically minded children may like to stand Mr. Potato outside; wild birds enjoy nibbling his hair. When Mr. Potato has begun to look bad, remove the pins and styrofoam and give him a decent burial in the compost heap.

Sacred Gardens

Throughout history, man has given gifts to God and the saints in gratitude for favors received. Those given in payment of a promise or a vow are known as *ex votos*. Artistic expressions are an intrinsic part of the human experience, and of all the countless works of art, many are created by folk artists. Just as kings and the wealthy have built shrines and churches, many folk artists throughout the world have created simple shrines to honor God and his saints, or as ex votos. Homemade shrines can be found in gardens and yards throughout the world.

Mr. Potato

The Sacred Gardens of New Waverly, Texas

The A.G. Blozek family of New Waverly, Texas, has created over 65 folk art shrines on the three-and-a-half acres of land near their home. When their oldest son was a child, he was diagnosed with a severe medical problem. In gratitude to God for his miraculous recovery, they began making simple shrines around their home. The bishop of their diocese blessed the gardens in 1972.

Each of the shrines is unique, and each tells a story. A giant outdoor rosary is made of large stones; each Our Father bead weighs about a ton, and the rosary encircles a garden 35-by-75 feet. As with many folk artists, the Blozeks used many items thrown away by others. Old bathtubs have been turned into grottos, and culverts form columns in some of the grottos. The statue of St. Isidore is flanked by a real plow. Metal flowers ornamenting one shrine to Our Lady have been made from cast-off metal drums. Hand-cut wooden signs identify the various shrines, and several have been made as memorials to deceased friends, or by different groups in the area. Beautiful landscaping, stately pines, and glowing flowers form a lush background for the concrete images and handcrafted shrines of the gardens. Every part of the gardens invokes the majesty of the Creator, and the love of the simple and humble Czech couple who created them in thanksgiving.

Mexican-American Yard Shrines

Throughout the American Southwest, Mexican-American artists have communicated their gratitude and devotion through the medium of yard and garden shrines, known as "*nichos*" or "*grutas*." A nicho is often built as the result of a promise made to a favorite saint, although some simply make a statement that the home is a Catholic one.

When the nicho or gruta is built in gratitude, the petitioner asks the saint for some form of intervention during a life crisis (such as a debilitating illness or dangerous military service) and promises to dedicate a shrine to that saint if his prayers are granted. The completion of this vow is a serious and binding obligation. Some nichos are found in front yards and are the focal point of the landscaping, or subtly incorporated as one element of the home's surroundings. Others are placed in private places in the back or side of the house and become areas for private meditation.

Nichos are made in a variety of sizes and generally have a border that forms a boundary for the sacred area. Borders are often made of bricks, rocks, or plants. The enclosure for the statue or icon is made of a variety of materials. Cement and exterior-grade wood are among the most popular materials used and these coverings are generally either arched or have pitched roofs, giving them the appearance of a cave or a miniature house. Some nichos are made of castaway materials and old-fashioned cast-iron tubs set on end are common.

Not all of the yard shrines have a covering or shell. Often a statue is elevated on some sort of a pedestal, such as a post or a bird bath.

Although plants and flowers are the most common, decorations for nichos are unlimited. Christmas decorations, ribbon, and seashells are often found on these home shrines. Marbles, glass, candles, lights, figurines, and ceramic tiles are also commonly used and, although the nicho is usually dedicated to a single saint, images of other saints and crucifixes may be added. Since the nicho often becomes a place of prayer and meditation for the entire family, other decorations and objects may be added. *Milagros*, small metal *ex votos* in the shape of people, animals, or hearts, are sometimes attached to the hands of the statue. Sometimes, photos of the loved one who was helped are incorporated in the nicho.

The icons used in home garden shrines are usually statues made from concrete, plaster, ceramic, or plastic. Some shrines do not use a statue but use a two-dimensional representation of a favorite saint instead. There are favorite saints depicted in these home shrines; in the American Southwest the most prevalent is the Virgin of Guadalupe. Sometimes shrines in her honor also contain the figure of Blessed Juan Diego, just as the shrines in honor of

Our Lady of Lourdes and Our Lady of Fatima also contain the image of the seers. The majority of the saints honored in the nichos are officially recognized by the Catholic Church, although sometimes "folk saints" such as Don Pedrito Jaramillo can be found.

Even the process of acquiring the icon or statue is sometimes a special part of fulfilling the promise, and families often make a pilgrimage to a famous shrine in order to obtain a replica of the particular Virgin or saint they want to honor.

A number of other names are given to the outdoor housing of a religious icon by Americans of Hispanic descent. A nicho simply is a "niche," and these can be found near the doors or address markers for many homes. Gruta, in English, means "grotto," and most enclosed yard shrines take the form of small grottos, or caves, although some seem to be tiny churches and are called *capillitas*, or little chapels. *Descansos*, or stopping places, are small shrines built by the side of the road and generally commemorate the place of death where the soul has left the body although some of these are also made in completion of a *manda*, which is a legacy or bequest.

The Holy Child of the Doves

Deep in the center of Mexico, in an old airplane hangar, a small statue of the Christ Child is the focus of a devotion that is spreading a message of Christian faith, hope, and love throughout the country and past its frontiers. Known as the Holy Child of the Doves, the little thaumaturge welcomes pilgrims and promotes clear doctrine.

The modernistic emblem of the Sanctuary of the Holy Child of the Doves is, itself, a lesson. A cross and a circle are symbolic of Christ as true man and true God. At the base of the cross is an arrow with a dove, representing the person who revolves about Jesus, making Jesus the center of his life. Many also find a message in the dove, symbolic of the Holy Spirit, the dove that brought hope and comfort to Noah, and the dove of peace.

Father Clemente of St. Joseph (1879-1974) was the initiator and fervent promoter of the devotion. When he was a young Carmelite priest in Spain, one day in 1923 a pious lady gave him a small statue of the Child Jesus holding two doves.

Assigned as a missionary, Father Clemente carried the gracious little sculpture wherever he went. Like a companion, it traveled with him across Spain, to Colombia, Cartagena, Leiva, and finally to Mexico in 1940. The

Holy Child of the Doves inspired his pastoral labors, and wherever he went, Father Clemente infused a great love of the Child Jesus among the people. At one time Father Clemente became gravely ill and petitioned the Christ Child before his little image for a cure in order to continue his missionary labors. His prayer was granted and he spent a fruitful and faithful life in Mexico.

When Father Clemente entered Mexico in 1940, foreign priests were prohibited from exercising their priestly ministry, so he had to adopt disguises and utilize pious deceptions. Working hard for the people with holy tranquility, Father Clemente was able to escape persecution.

He became master of novices at the Carmel in Mexico City.

The novices soon realized the great love and devotion their novice master had for the Child Jesus. Father Clemente always carried the image with him, and when he went to preach or give spiritual retreats to the religious houses, the image presided over the celebrations. Although the devotion to the Child of the Doves initially developed in the Carmelite environment, it rapidly became known outside and the image began to be exposed to public veneration.

The devotion was approved by the Archbishop of Mexico in 1944, and in 1945 the image was placed on a special altar in the Church of Our Lady of Carmel, the church where the Carmelites began their apostolic labors on the American continent in 1585. Today, the annual feast of the Holy Child of the Doves is celebrated on January 7 in Mexico. When a number of devotions in Mexico were suppressed because they had been altered with the presence of superstitious practices, devotion to the Holy Child of the Doves was included. Father Clemente immediately went to its defense, and an authorization of ratification allowed it to continue. The dedicated priest passed his final years at the Carmel of Celaya, Guanajuato, where he closed his eyes to this world in 1974.

In 1973, near the town of Guadalupe, Zacatecas, a devout family, the Villalobos, lived at the small Rancho of San Carlos. Doña Catalina Villalobos became seriously ill. Two of her aunts brought her a small medal of the Holy Child of the Doves and together they petitioned Him for a cure. Miraculously, Doña Catalina was completely cured.

In gratitude, Doña Catalina commissioned a prominent sculptor to make an image of the Holy Child, which was blessed and put in the family oratory. A copy of Father Clemente's original, the Zacatecas image has a third dove near his left foot, added at Doña Catalina's request. A beautiful work of art, the little image of Jesus seems to radiate peace and faith.

From the small family oratory, a spark was lighted which fired the devotion in concentric circles and began to spread it across a large part of the country. The cure of Doña Catalina was only one of the first signs; soon many other signal favors began to occur. The image gained a reputation as a miracle worker, a *thaumaturge*.

By 1976, so many people were coming to the little family oratory that the Archbishop of Zacatecas authorized the construction of a new chapel. In 1989, the parish priest of Our Lady of Loreto church in Guadalupe, Zacatecas, was placed in charge of the chapel of the Holy Child of the Doves. Later that year, the Bishop closed the chapel and ordered the image translated to a temporary shrine closer to the highway, made in the hangar of an old airport near the small town of Palomitas. Father Gustavo Guijarro Montes was appointed as the shrine's first rector.

In his provisional temple, the veneration of the Holy Child of the Doves has increased and accelerated. Devotees, primarily from the central states of Mexico, come to the shrine to give thanks for favors received or to implore His protection and help. Hearts are drawn as if to a magnet by the graceful little image. In the same manner that the multitudes followed Jesus, pilgrims come to a humble shrine near a poor town to receive the Word and to see His miracles. Prominently displayed in the office and gift shop of the shrine are study Bibles. The intriguing little book on the history of the devotion, written by the rector, is a commonsense recitation of the history and a catechistic basis for the devotion, rooted in sound theology and replete with biblical references.

Even with such a relatively new devotion in the Church, pious legends exist. In the words of the shrine's rector, "popular psychology is very prone to mix elements of fantasy and mystery with historical truth. Legends telling of a supernatural origin of the image abound and many of the pilgrims want to know about the apparitions. Although legends spice a popular story, the true history is raised up in truth. At the bottom, we need to accept with love and faith what the image *represents*. This is the most important."

The doves symbolize purity, innocence, and simplicity. "Be simple like the doves," said Jesus (Matthew 10:16). In the case of the doves of the Child Jesus, according to Father Clemente, the doves represent the souls of the "simple, the pure, the loved ones of Christ that want to live in His love; the ones that look for the truth and for peace in charity." The child has imprisoned the doves in his hands next to His heart in order to show us the protection and the prodigious love He has for us.

Commemorate the Holy Child by building a bird feeder to attract our feathered friends. Although the Holy Child of the Doves is not well known in the United States and statues of him are rare, any representation of Christ as a child will do. Perhaps the most popular and easily available is the Infant of Prague; in the Southwest, the Infant of the Atocha representations are common.

Holy Child Bird Feeder

See the diagram below for assembly details.

First, cut a 10½" base from the 1"x6" scrap lumber.

Cut 2 sides from the 1"x6" that are 6¾" along the front and 5½" along the back.

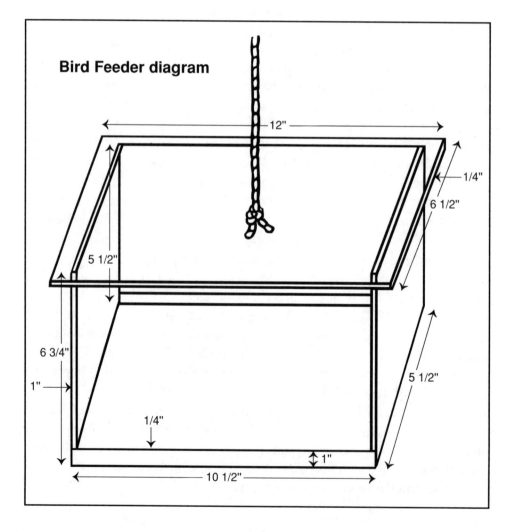

Cut a 12" x 6½" piece from the plywood for a top.

Cut 2 pieces of plywood 1" by 10½" for the rails.

Drill 2 small starter holes on each of the short sides of the base and attach side boards vertically with screws. Attach top with 2 screws on each of the short sides. Remember to drill starter holes first. Attach rails to front and back of base of feeder with a screw on each end.

Find the balance point in the top by holding the feeder on a finger. Mark the point and drill a hole to receive a piece of rope. Make a knot in one end of the rope and thread through the hole to hang.

Drill a starter hole and run a 2" screw up from the bottom. Center the small statue over the screw, inside the feeder. Attach the statue with hot glue for greater stability.

Make a Gourd Birdhouse

The first birdhouses in North America may well have been made by early Native Americans from gourds. Depending on the size of the entrance hole, where the birdhouse is hung, the size of the gourd, and what part of the country you live in, gourd birdhouses will attract a variety of birds. This project can be a good family project, although a lot of patience is called for; the project can't be done in a single sitting. City dwellers who don't have convenient trees to hang their houses in can still enjoy the imaginative project and can complete their birdhouse with an artificial bird and nest to grace a window.

You can obtain gourds at the grocery store in the fall. You may even want to grow your own. Gourds require a long growing season and a temperate climate, so if you decide to grow your

Supplies needed
saw
drill
1, 2" screw
12, ¾" screws
1"x6" scrap lumber (treated lumber is best)
¼" plywood scraps
length of rope
small plastic or ceramic statue of the Christ child with a hole in the bottom
hot-glue gun

Supplies needed
1 gourd per house, at least 5" in diameter and 6" to 8" tall
small gourd or gourd pieces
sharp utility knife
ice pick
piece of wire about 12" long
sandpaper
paint — spray enamel of any color; acrylics for highlights
hot-glue gun

own and you live in a cooler climate, you should start your plants inside in the fall. Follow the seed packet's directions for your area of the country.

Placing the entrance holes correctly can mean the difference between providing a safe habitat and killing baby birds. If you make the opening too high, rain will come in and drown the fledglings; if you make it too low, they may tumble out. Cut the entry hole exactly perpendicular to the vertical axis of the gourd when it is suspended, along the outermost part of the curve pointing neither upward or downward. We used a spare piece of gourd to form the base for our covered entry. To copy our house, follow the instructions below, or let your imagination guide you in making your own.

If you are working with gourds that are thoroughly dry, you will need to drill the beginning holes and use a face mask because gourd dust can get in your nose and bother you. We worked with gourds fresh from the grocery which were not dry.

Using a sharp knife, cut the entry hole. Depending on the type of bird you want to attract, the hole should be 1" in diameter for house wrens, 1⅛" for other types of wrens and chickadees. Swallows and purple martins can be attracted to gourd birdhouses, but you would need a much larger gourd for these.

With an ice pick, punch about three holes in the bottom of the gourd for drainage. Make a hole at the top to insert your wire hanger.

Using a spoon, scrape out the seeds and some of the pulp. We spread the seeds on a paper towel to save them for next year's planting. Next, allow your gourd to dry thoroughly. This would normally take over a week, but you can get a head start by putting your gourd in a warm (200°) oven for several hours.

When your gourd is thoroughly

Gourd Birdhouses

dry, cut a piece of gourd for a canopy over the entrance. Use sandpaper to smooth the rough edges of the canopy and to remove any jagged spots on the entry hole.

Make a loop in the end of your wire and thread the other end up through the hole at the top of the birdhouse. Using your hot-glue gun, affix the canopy over the entry hole. Add a spot of glue at the top where the wire comes out of the gourd to completely waterproof the hole.

Hang your birdhouse outside on a convenient limb or other projection while you spray paint it with several light coats of paint. We used an old can of green enamel and a can of the paint that simulates stone to achieve a mottled effect.

We used a hot-glue gun and a variety of materials to finish the canopies of our gourd houses. For the tallest house, we glued on cornhusks all around the top of the house like a straw roof. Leaves from a silver-dollar eucalyptus tree were glued in a semi-circular pattern over the porch of another. Lichen-covered twigs finished the canopy of the third house. Dried leaves, grasses, and other materials from your yard can make interesting roofs and verandas. Finish your gourd house with several coats of clear spray. Use your wire to hang them in a convenient tree in hopes of attracting a boarder.

Quick Basket Bird Feeder

You can make an easy, inexpensive bird feeder from a basket-style paper plate holder and string. Color up the feeder, and your garden, with a handful of silk flowers, if you like.

Cut 2 pieces of nylon twine 42" long each. Work an end of 1 string through the edge of the plate holder at least ¼" to ½" in from the rim. Tie the twine in a tight knot and carefully burn the ends to keep them from fraying.

Thread the string through the washer and tie it onto the exact opposite side of the holder. Again, burn the ends.

Tie the end of the other string halfway around the edge between the first and second knots. Pass this string through the washer and through the opposite side of the rim. This time, before you tie

Supplies needed

scissors

nylon twine

small washer

paper plate basket-style holder

cigarette lighter or match

Optional:

hot-glue gun

ribbon

silk flowers

large paper clip

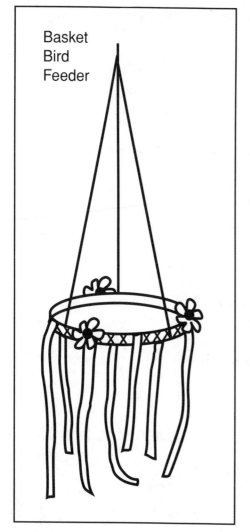

Basket
Bird
Feeder

the knot, hold the washer and let the basket hang freely to make certain you have all four of the support strings as close to the same length as possible. Tie your knot and burn the ends.

Cut a length of twine a few inches long. Wrap this string tightly around the other four strings several times, as close as possible to the washer, and knot and burn the ends. Cut off any excess string.

Fold the center section of the large paper clip out and down to make an s-shaped hook. Slip one end of the hook through the washer and hang your feeder in a tree with the other end.

If you have a handful of leftover silk flowers and leaves and some ribbon, glue the ribbon and flowers near the support strings on the edge of the basket. The cheapest "silk" flowers, which are usually made of a synthetic material, will stay bright and colorful for several months. Hair ribbon, florist ribbon, or nylon ribbon is the best choice; paper ribbon will not hold up.

Mary Gardens

May Is Mary's Month

"O Mary, we crown thee with blossoms today, Queen of the Angels, Queen of the May."

Many American Catholics remember the beautiful May crowning ceremonies of a few years ago: girls dressed in frothy white dresses and boys with slicked-down hair and grown-up ties processed with songs, rosary beads, and a floral crown for the parish statue of the Virgin.

Today, a number of parishes and schools across the nation are reinstituting this beautiful custom. Along with their human mothers, they again honor their heavenly mother.

May is traditionally held to be the month of Our Lady. But why?

Although May is a contraction of the name Mary, the month was probably named for Maia Majesta, the Roman goddess of grain. The people of ancient Rome celebrated the first day of May by honoring Flora, the goddess of flowers. She was represented by a small statue wreathed in garlands. A procession of singers and dancers carried the statue past a sacred, blossom-decked tree. Later, festivals of this kind spread to other parts of Europe, reaching their height of popularity in England during the Middle Ages. Dances around a flower-bedecked Maypole were common, and the festivities often blossomed into riotous and wild occasions. Often a May queen was chosen as part of the festivities.

Devotions to Our Lady on the first days of May date from medieval times, when St. Philip Neri (sixteenth century) began the custom of decorating the statue of the Virgin with spring flowers. Annibale Dionisi, an Italian Jesuit, proposed devotions to Mary throughout the entire month. Just as happened with other pre-Christian customs and festivals, the Church incorporated the pre-Christian May celebrations and gave them a Christian dimension. May began to be celebrated in honor of Our Lady with much the same type of festivities, including floral tributes and processions.

It wasn't until the early part of the nineteenth century, however, that devotion to Mary during this month received its greatest impetus. During the entire century, dedication of the month in the Virgin's honor began to take hold for a number of reasons.

In 1809, Pope Pius VII was made a captive by Napoleon and deported to France, where he remained in exile until May 24, 1814. After five years of imprisonment, he re-entered Rome amid the loud acclaim of the populace, and was re-instated on his throne. In gratitude for her help, he instituted a feast in honor of Mary, Help of Christians, and wrote a memo in 1815 enriching the public May devotions with indulgences. These were confirmed by the Sacred Congregation for Indulgences in 1822.

The hundred-plus years from 1854 to the close of the Second Vatican Council in 1965 were the most prolific ever in doctrinal development in Mariology. No other period in Catholic history is comparable. One reason for this was the reaction against rationalism in modern times. When critics of the Faith challenged the foundations of belief in Christ's divinity, the response of the Church was to reaffirm it, to defend the actions of the councils of Nicea and Chalcedon, and to safeguard the dignity of Mary, Mother of God. The Church was also acting against the anti-religious principles of Communism and other political evils. Popes Pius IX, Leo XIII, Pius XI, and Pius XII all wrote documents condemning Communism.

Devotion to Mary also grew as the role of women became more prominent in private and professional life, and their unique position was threatened by a rampant secularism that exploited them for its own ends. Faith in Mary's dignity had an ennobling influence on the life and literature of Western thought. Mary's role as the highest symbol of womanhood is significant, but from the Catholic standpoint valuable only if firmly rooted in Christian revelation.

A series of Marian doctrines was presented to the Church's faithful during this time in history to assure them that what they had been practicing was divinely authorized and that their piety was founded on the principles of faith.

The apparitions at LaSalette and Lourdes took place during the middle of the century, and since then there has ever been interest in the apparitions of Mary, the Mother of God.

On December 8, 1854, Pope Pius IX issued the document *Ineffabilis Deus*, in which he proclaimed the Immaculate Conception. During the pontificate of Pope Pius XI, the Penitentiary Apostolic on March 28, 1933, again reaffirmed the May devotions and further enriched them with indulgences. Mary's Assumption was defined as dogma by Pius XII in 1950.

A feast in honor of Mary, Queen of All Saints, was established by Pope Pius XII in 1954 to commemorate Mary's high dignity as queen of heaven, angels, and men. This title sums up all the other titles preceding it, and is the crowning of all the privileges, virtues, and merits of Mary. Universal observance of the memorial was ordered near the close of a Marian year observed in connection with the centenary of the proclamation of the dogma of the Immaculate Conception and four years after the proclamation of the dogma of the Assumption. Originally celebrated on May 31, the memorial is now observed on August 22.

Today the ancient feast of the Visitation is celebrated on May 31, and completes the May devotions to Our Lady. The memorial commemorates Mary's visit to her cousin Elizabeth after the Annunciation and before the birth of John the Baptist, the precursor of Christ (Luke 1:39-57). The observance originated in the Franciscan Order in medieval times and was extended throughout the Church by Pope Urban VI in 1389. One of the feasts of the Incarnation, this feast recalls the Magnificat, one of the few New Testament canticles which acknowledges the unique gifts of God to Mary because of her role in the redemptive work of Christ.

Pope John Paul II has always cultivated a strong devotion to Mary. He proclaimed 1987-1988 a Marian year. At the time of his first apostolic visit to the United States, he reminded all Americans, "This woman becomes also, by association with her Son, the sign of contradiction to the world, and at the same time the sign of hope, who all generations shall call blessed."

Author John Rotelle, O.S.A., tells us, "As we prepare for our entry into the twenty-first century, what will devotion to Mary bring? No one knows. However, we do know that her most venerated and revered title will last from century to century: Mary, the Mother of God, Theotokos."

Mary Gardens Honor Our Lady

In medieval times, a charming custom arose of planting "Mary gardens," small gardens consisting of flowers and herbs ascribed by love and legend as special tributes to the Blessed Virgin. Around the middle of the present century, this custom was revived in many places in Europe and the United States.

If you would like to set aside a portion of your own garden as a Mary garden, some ideas are outlined below. But use your creativity to set up your own special tribute to Our Lady.

Such gardens combine nature with folk tales to pay tribute to the Madonna and to illustrate what the Church and Scripture teach about her.

In a typical Mary garden, a statue of the Virgin occupies the place of honor. Statues of concrete, molded plastic, or ceramic are suitable for use

A Mary Garden

outside, and are generally available at your local garden store. The image can be centered in the garden or placed in a grotto or shelter against the wall. A simple wooden triangle makes a nice shelter for use on a wooden fence and can also serve as a bird feeder. Bricks or rocks stacked in a semicircle make a good background for a larger statue. Sometimes, a birdbath or bubbling fountain is placed in front of the statue. These can be elaborate ones purchased from your garden center, or something as simple as a large bowl set into the soil and rimmed with rocks.

The original Mary gardens may have been a Christian outgrowth of pre-Christian nature rites celebrating spring. After the long, cold winter, our ancestors were filled with joy over the appearance of new growth in the spring, and they attributed special powers of protection and healing to them. They planted spring flower gardens and brought early-blooming plants into their homes, decorating themselves and their rooms with garlands and wreaths of flowers and blossoms. Although the Mary garden is usually geared toward springtime growth, careful selection of plants could make it beautiful every season of the year. Including both flowering plants for beauty and functional plants, such as herbs, makes the garden both aesthetically pleasing and practical.

It is wise to make a complete plan for your garden before starting to plant. Gardeners should not forget to check the hardiness and suitability of each plant for the area's climate.

Roses have been associated with Mary from the earliest times. The word "rosary" originally meant a rose garden, but later was used in the sense of "rose garland." Such garlands were decorations and awards to the ancient Romans, who were very familiar with cultivated roses.

St. Dominic and the Dominicans in the thirteenth century began the spread of the devotion known as the Rosary, a garland of prayers in honor of the Virgin. Three colors of roses are especially appropriate in a Mary garden: red roses to symbolize the sorrows of Our Lady, white to symbolize her joys, and yellow to symbolize and herald her glories.

Add roses to your Mary garden, not only for their beauty, but also for their usefulness. The petals can be saved for potpourri and the hips are a good source of vitamin C. The ancient herbalists used roses in many ways.

Marigolds are sometimes called "Mary's bud." An old legend says the dresses of the Virgin Mary were adorned with this flower, and it has been used to decorate her shrines for the feast of the Annunciation and during the month of May. The flower is hardy in most parts of the United States, although many object to the strong odor of its blossoms. It is a helpful plant and keeps many garden pests from attacking. In ancient times, marigold flowers were often dried and used in soups and broths. It was used medicinally by herbalists and forms the basis for a yellow dye used in cosmetics.

Columbine and trefoil are said to have sprung forth from the earth at the touch of Mary's foot, and consequently bear the popular names "Our Lady's shoes" or "Our Lady's slippers." The yellow lady's slipper (*Cypripedium*) is also known as American valerian.

The common name for a number of other plants marks them as property of Our Lady. Legend tells us that Our Lady used Lady's bedstraw (*Galium verum*) as one of the cradle herbs added to the hay in the manger of Bethlehem. Lady's mantle (*Alchemilla vulgaris*) seemed to the sixteenth-century botanist Tragus to have leaves resembling Our Lady's robe. The flat seed-pouches of lady's purse (*Capsella bursa-pastoris*) resemble a common leather purse. In America, this plant is commonly called shepherd's purse, and small birds are particularly fond of its seed.

Lady's seal (*Polygonatum multiflorum*) may have received its name from the flat, round scars on the rootstocks resembling a seal. *Spiranthes autumnalis*, a fall-blooming plant, must have impressed an ancient herbalist with the spiral arrangement of its flowers, which he likened to Our Lady's curls when he named the plant "Our Lady's tresses."

The stately and dignified lily has been associated from ancient times with Jesus and Mary. It is an old and traditional symbol of innocence, purity, and virginity. The Madonna lily (*lilium candidum*) was dedicated by the Church to the Madonna in the early days of Christianity and was often employed in connection with the celebrations of the Visitation of the Blessed Virgin. Lily-of-the-valley is also called Our Lady's tears. The foxglove grows in moist and shady places and blooms in many colors with clusters of little bells. In medieval times, the plant was known as "Our Lady's thimbles," "virgin's glove," or "gloves of Our Lady." The plant is the source of digitalis, a medicine commonly used for heart problems.

The snowdrop is the first herald of spring in Europe. It often blossoms as early as the first week in February, sometimes springing up through patches of snow. Little bouquets of this flower are the first floral tribute of the year at the shrines of the Madonna, and the flower is a popular emblem of Mary's purity and freedom from sin.

Violets are a symbol of Mary's humility and are said to have blossomed outside her window when she spoke the words, "Behold, I am the handmaid of the Lord" (Luke 1:38). Tradition says when the angel left this humble virgin, he blessed the little flowers as he passed, endowing them with the most tender and most beautiful fragrance of all plants.

Hundreds of other plants and herbs are connected with the Virgin in various ways and traditions. The fig was said to have sheltered the Holy Family on their journey into Egypt to escape the wrath of Herod. American wormseed (*Chenopodium anthelminticum*) was marketed under the name "*Herba Sancti Maria*" in the early days of this century as an expectorant and a medicine for asthma sufferers. Angelica was associated with the springtime festival of the Annunciation. Costmary was known as "*Herbe Sainte Marie*" in France, and was widely used during the Middle Ages as a medicine and as a spice and a preservative. The cowslip, whose pendant flowers suggested a bunch of keys, was dedicated to the Virgin in northern Europe and called "Our Lady's keys," or "key of heaven."

Great mullein (*Verbascum thapsus*) has been known as "Our Lady's flannel" or "Our Lady's candle." Those who are prone to plant allergies, however, know this plant as goldenrod.

Spearmint, rosemary, tansy, and thyme are four aromatic herbs dedicated to Our Lady that would make good additions to a Mary garden.

Spearmint was particularly dedicated to the Virgin Mary, and its common names include "Our Lady's mint," "*Herba Santa Maria*," and "*Menthe de Notre Dame*."

Mint was one of the favorite strewing herbs in the Middle Ages; it was strewn on the floors of churches and banquet halls to furnish a pleasant odor. It was also used by the monks medicinally and culinarily. Modern housewives value it for two of its properties: it is useful in counteracting the smell of tobacco, and mice cannot stand the odor.

According to legend, the rosemary plants originally had white blossoms, and these turned blue, Mary's color, in reward for the service it offered when Our Lady looked for a bush on which to spread her Child's tiny clothes when she washed the garments on the way to Egypt. An old superstition says the plant will never grow taller than the height of Christ.

Tansy was another of the strewing herbs dedicated to the Virgin and connected with traditions at Easter. Archbishops and bishops played handball with men of their congregations and a tansy cake was the reward for the victors. The cakes, made from the young leaves of the plant mixed with eggs, were thought to purify the body after the limited foods of Lent.

A Mary Garden in Miniature

Apartment dwellers who do not have the luxury of a large yard can still honor Our Lady with a Mary garden in miniature. The completed garden will do well for some time in a bright window. If you use it as a table centerpiece, set it outside when it begins to look limp.

Select a container for your dish garden — clay, ceramic, or plastic will work. Place a layer of charcoal in the bottom of the dish, which will serve to catch any excess water and will keep the soil smelling sweet. Charcoal that is used in aquarium filters works well, or simply break up some of your barbecue charcoal briquettes. Add a good quality potting soil. Use a statue of the Virgin that corresponds in size with your container. Small, inexpensive plastic and ceramic statues are available at your local religious goods store if you don't already have one.

Arrange plants around the statue with the taller ones in the back. Plants that grow rapidly can be trimmed with scissors.

In our Mary dish-garden we used a miniature rosebush, a mini violet, spearmint, and marigolds. African violets would be beautiful, too. Rosemary, an herb dedicated to Our Lady, can even be trained over a miniature trellis. Your local nursery can suggest a variety of plants that grow well together.

Mary Gardens Today

The first Mary garden in the United States is believed to be that at St. Joseph's Church in Woods Hole, Massachusetts. In 1932, Mrs. Frances Crane Lillie , a summer resident of Woods Hole, researched herbs and plants with old religious names that symbolized the Virgin Mary. She planted a selection of these in a garden at St. Joseph's Church. After the first year of Mrs. Lillie's "Garden of Our Lady," revisions were made and in 1933 it was replanted with 48 specimens which were planted around a commissioned statue of the Virgin Mary in a cross-shaped bed.

After twice being destroyed by hurricanes, the garden has been restored to its original planting plan. The restoration was prompted by the rediscovery of the garden's historical uniqueness and significance by the parishioners in the course of the research undertaken for the writing of a commemorative history for the centennial of the parish.

The Woods Hole garden was the inspiration for the foundation of an organization called Mary's Gardens, which was founded in Philadelphia in 1951 by two young businessmen, Edward A.G. McTague and John S. Stokes, Jr. The aim of the non-profit group is to revive the medieval practice of cultivating gardens of herbs and flowers which have Marian names and to research the hundreds of plants symbolic of the life, mysteries, and privileges of the Blessed Virgin Mary. The founders hope that people will plant Mary gardens as a prayerful, religious work of stewardship for God's flower riches and artistry with devotion, praise, meditation, and commitment. Research by this foundation has resulted in a list of over a thousand herb, flower, shrub, and tree names that are symbolic of Mary.

Proposed initially for home gardens, Mary gardens soon became established also at schools, parishes, burial plots, institutions, and shrines. In 1983, a Mary garden was even established inside prison walls at the Idaho State Penitentiary. The traditional image of Our Lady of Guadalupe was painted by a prisoner-artist and a shrine was built around it made of rocks dug from the prison yard, flowers, and grass.

Some of the better known Mary gardens today are those at Our Lady's national shrines at Knock, Ireland, and Akita, Japan; at the Artane Oratory of the Resurrection in Dublin; and in the cloister planting of Lincoln Cathedral in England. In the United States, there is a beautiful Mary garden at St. Mary's Parish in Annapolis, Maryland, adjacent to the historic Carroll House.

Today, the work of Mary's Gardens is continued by an informal association of committed persons in Pennsylvania, Massachusetts, Maryland, Ohio, and Dublin, Ireland. In 1995, the organization opened an Internet web site to make their literature and photographs available in electronic form. The address is http://www.mgardens.org.

Roses From Our Lady

Our Lady has appeared to believers worldwide. She has often been seen wearing roses, and sometimes she uses created things to emphasize her message.

In Mexico, in 1531, Our Lady of Guadalupe placed rare Castillian roses in Juan Diego's *tilma* (cloak) as a sign of the truth of her presence. When Juan arrived at the bishop's residence with the flowers Our Lady had gathered, she had also miraculously left her picture on his humble garment.

In 1858 at Lourdes, France, Our Lady appeared standing on a rose bush and with golden roses on her feet. Only the seer, young Bernadette Soubirous, could see and hear Our Lady, so the crowds who had gathered thought it strange to see Bernadette scrabbling in the mud at the grotto of Massabielle. Some shouted out that she was insane, but as the child dug deeper, a bubbling sound was heard, and water from an underground and previously hidden spring began to flow forth. Today, this miraculous water continues to flow and pilgrims flock from around the world to bathe in the healing stream.

From the end of the seventeenth century, Vietnamese Catholics suffered a number of severe persecutions, and in the mid-eighteenth century alone over 100,000 Catholics were martyred. The first persecution of Catholics in central Vietnam, which began around 1698, was so severe that many of the people fled to a remote jungle area in the mountains near Lavang, hoping for freedom to practice their religion, as well as to save their lives. One evening, as the community was reciting the Rosary together, there was an apparition of a beautiful lady holding a little child in her arms, with angels surrounding her. The lady was dressed simply, but wore a crown, and the people recognized her as the Queen of Heaven. Our Lady spoke to the people in the loving tones of a mother, encouraging and comforting them. Displaying a tender concern for her children, she taught the people how to make medicines from the plants and herbs that grew in the area, and promised her protection to those who would come to that particular site to pray. The people built a simple church of leaves and rice straw and dedicated it to their Mother Mary. Through other persecutions, the Lavang area continued to be a sanctuary for oppressed Catholics, although at one time 30 Catholics were martyred right at the door of the church, which was burned. Later, a new brick church was built in its place.

At Fatima, Portugal, the sun appeared to dance. In the convent at Akita, Japan, there are soothing mineral waters to bathe in. At Betania, Venezuela, pilgrims report large flocks of blue butterflies. A flock of white doves, flying in pairs, presaged the apparitions in Cairo, Egypt. In speaking of the apparitions of Our Lady, we are dealing with the supernatural, yet time and again she emphasizes and returns us to the beauty of the natural world we live in.

Roses for Our Lady — The Dominican Rosary

The labors and the prayers of the Dominican Order have contributed greatly to the diffusion of the Rosary and the vast influence is has exercised for good from the fifteenth century to our current times, although its history and origin are shrouded in the mists of time. That the rosary is a prayer of the people, useful for simple and learned alike, is proved by the many pronouncements of the popes and the experience of all who are familiar with it. It is one of the most beautiful meditations on the fundamentals of our Faith and one of the prime sacramentals of the Western Church. But why do we call this string of prayer beads a rosary?

The word "*rosarius*" means a garland or bouquet of roses, and it was often used in a figurative sense, such as in the title of a book to denote an anthology or collection. An early legend traveled all over Europe and connected the name with Our Lady. The legend tells that Our Lady was once seen to take rosebuds from the lips of a young monk when he was reciting Hail Marys, and weave them into a garland which she placed upon her head. A German metrical version of this legend from the thirteenth century is still extant. The words "corona" or "chaplet" suggests the same idea as rosarium. The old English name found in Chaucer and elsewhere was a "pair of beads," where the word "beads" originally meant prayers.

The beads of the rosary are a physical reminder of the repetitive prayers that form a background for contemplation and meditation. What better venue than a peaceful garden spot with the sight of its beautiful blooms and the heady odor of its perfume to tell our beads? The rosary, however, can be prayed in the garden in other ways besides clutching a string of beads in hand. When watering and nurturing the tender plants, the length of time needed to say an Ave allows just enough of the life-giving fluid to pour onto each plant on a hot summer day. A fruitful meditation could center on how prayer nourishes and strengthens our work. Cultivating around the plants, or pulling weeds for the time of a Hail Mary can produce the same results, reserving the Our Father for the most weed-choked or uncultivated plants.

Many gardeners use stones to mark off a rosary in their garden. Some make the stones large enough to step on, so that one can physically walk the way of the rosary. Others use pebbles to call to mind Our Lady near a particular part of their garden, sometimes the section reserved and known as a Mary garden.

Blessed Flowers

A pious custom in Dominican and some other churches on the Feast of the Holy Rosary is the blessing of roses. The rose is seen as a figure of the rosary and its mysteries.

The green leaves represent the Joyful Mysteries; the thorns of the bush stand for the Sorrowful Mysteries. The Glorious Mysteries are seen in the flowers.

The formula in the Roman Ritual for the blessing of the roses reads: "God, Creator and Preserver of mankind, deign to pour out Thy heavenly benediction upon these roses, which we offer to Thee through devotion and reverence for Our Lady of the Rosary. Grant that these roses, which are made by Thy Providence to yield an agreeable perfume for the use of men and women, may receive such a blessing by the sign of Thy holy cross that all the sick on whom they shall be laid and all who shall keep them in their houses may be cured of their ills; and that the devils may fly in terror from these dwellings, not daring to disturb Thy servants."

Roses and rose petals are often blessed in honor of one of the saints and used as sacramentals by the faithful. St. Rita of Cascia and St. Thérèse of Lisieux are two saints whose cults include blessing of rose petals.

Lilies are blessed on the feast of St. Anthony of Padua. As part of the ritual blessing, the priest prays: "You [God] in your great kindness have given them to man, and endowed them with a sweet fragrance to lighten the burden of the sick. Therefore, let them be filled with such power that, whether they are used by the sick, or kept in homes or other places, or devoutly carried on one's person, they may serve to drive out evil spirits, safeguard holy chastity, and turn away illness —— all this through the prayers of St. Anthony — and finally impart to your servants grace and peace; through Christ our Lord."

All sacramentals, including blessed flowers and their blessings, derive their efficacy chiefly from the intercessory power of the Church. The faithful's cooperation has a very large part to play if blessings are to attain their full promise, raising human thoughts and aspirations out of the realm of the profane and up to the realm of the sacred.

Make Stepping Stones

Supplies needed

cement

water

bucket for mixing

throw-away paper or plastic cups

stirring stick

molds — old margarine tubs, plastic pots, plastic containers, etc.

cardboard or newspaper to work on

clear glitter — optional

seashells, colored rocks, aquarium stones, etc. — optional

Almost every garden of any size needs stepping stones in one place or another. Here's the way to make some, and a way that even the smallest child in the family can help make something and be commemorated in the garden.

This is an outside project; cement in your drainpipes in the house would be the occasion for a plumber's visit!

Directions

Choose your molds and set them on the cardboard or paper. We found that the large (3 lb.) plastic margarine container made a nice size. The 5" plastic throw-away pots that plants come from the nursery in are also a good size. (If you use pots, wrap the bottom with a thick layer of aluminum foil so the cement will not drip out.) For different sizes and shapes, you can use almost any plastic container that has a flat bottom and smooth, straight up-and-down or slightly flared-out sides. The molds cannot be used for food again, so choose old ones you don't care for.

In an old bucket, mix your cement and water in a 2 to 1 ratio. We used 10 plastic cups (6 oz.) of cement to 5 cups water to make 5 stones, 4½" in diameter and about 2" thick. (We used plain cement. If you are using a commercial product with aggregate such as Qwikcrete or

Redicrete, use the amount of water specified on the bag.)

Stir to mix thoroughly; your mixture should be about as thick as cake batter. Pour your mixture into the molds to a depth of 1½" to 2". Tap the sides of your mold as you would a cake pan full of batter to remove air bubbles. Try not to shake much of your "batter" up onto the side of your mold.

At this point you can "salt" the top of your stones with a light sprinkling of clear glitter if you wish. When dry, the glitter will give a hint of sparkle to your stones.

Stepping Stones with handprints

Allow your stepping stones to set for about 45 minutes to 1 hour. Concrete cures at a rate that varies depending on the heat, humidity, and sea level. We made a 2" test pour in a small plastic cup, and used it to determine when our cement was ready to mark.

When your cement has set to the consistency of heavy mud, carefully hold a baby's foot and press it into the cement, or help a small child press their hand into the cement. Wash hands and feet off immediately. It's best to use an outside hose over the grass. Remember the plumber!

Allow your cement to continue drying for at least 4 hours before unmolding. Carefully pull the sides of the mold away from the cement all the way around to loosen. Some molds will be more flexible than others; you can't move the sides very far, this is just to break any seal. Turn the pot over, and holding your hand over the top to catch the stone, tap the bottom of the mold. Your stone should pop out into your hand easily.

At this point, using the sharp tip of a nail file or a nail, you can write the child's name or the date on the side of your stone. Brush off loose crumbs with your finger.

Put the unmolded stone on your cardboard or paper and allow it to continue to cure for about 24 hours until it is completely hard and dry.

If you do not want to make hand or foot prints on your stones, you can decorate the top with small seashells, colored rocks, or glass aquarium stones. Decorate the tops of the stones when the cement has set enough to hold their weight, about the time we suggest making the prints.

Use your finished stones in your flowerbeds wherever you need them, or line a path with them. You can even make a "stepping rosary" with them.

Make A Stepping Rosary

You can form a unique "stepping rosary" with your cement stepping-stones. Choose round molds of two sizes: one for the Hail Mary beads and one for the Our Father beads. If your garden is large enough, you can make an entire rosary, or limit yourself to making a one-decade rosary.

A decade includes 10 Hail Mary beads and one Our Father bead. Make a cement cross to go with your stepping stones. Place your "stepping rosary" in a section of your garden planted with a low-growing herbal groundcover.

Make a Cement Cross

You will need: materials listed for the stepping stones, plus a rectangular corrugated cardboard box, a serrated knife, and a hot-glue gun with plenty of glue. A good size for your box is 9"x11½"x4½" if you want a cross to match your 5" stepping stones.

Using a serrated knife, cut off the top 4 flaps of your box. Cut the 2 longer flaps the same length as the shorter flaps. Next cut ⅓ of the length off the shorter 2 flaps.

Cutting your flaps in this manner will give you a nice proportion for your cross. We started with a box 9"x11½"x4½" deep ; thus our short flaps were originally 9" long. After cutting, we had 2 pieces of cardboard 9" long and 2 pieces of cardboard 6" long.

When you look into your box, you will see 2 short flaps on top of 2 long flaps that form the bottom. Bend the 2 short flaps up, put a few drops of hot glue between the flap and the side of the box, and hold the flap tight against the end of the box until the glue sets. The beauty of using hot glue is that it sets up rapidly; if you don't have a glue gun, you can tape the pieces firmly in place.

Bend your 2 shortest flaps exactly in half and glue them in the 2 corners of the end of the box to form squares. Try and make these as straight as possible. Make a bend ⅓ of the way down on the longer 2 flaps. Box off rectangles in the remaining 2 corners to form the rest of your cross outline.

We used 6, 6-oz. cups of cement to 3 cups of water, which made enough for our cross and 1 of margarine-tub stepping stones. We sprinkled on glitter and after a few hours we added some decorative stones to the top of the cross.

Don't let it fool you, though. You need to wait about 24 hours before trying to unmold the cross.

Make a Gardening Angel

Lorraine's Gardening Angel is just the thing to keep a good watch on your favorite flowerbed. Drill a hole for hanging and leave off the stake and she can even watch your indoor garden.

Directions

Using tracing paper, copy the pattern (found in the Appendix, page 149) onto the wood. Carefully cut out the pieces.

Drill holes where indicated.

Sand all pieces and wipe clean with tack cloth or rag.

Paint the angel's head, hands, and legs with flesh-colored paint. Paint her dress white. Daub her cheeks with thinned red or pink paint. Paint her shoes, the lines on her dress, and her collar with dark green. Make the flowers on her dress; Lorraine used yellow for the flowers with brown centers. Two black dots are the angel's eyes. Her mouth is a single red line, as shown in the illustration.

Paint the birdhouse to match the angel's dress.

When angel is completely dry, spray with several coats of matte spray paint, or clear spray to weatherproof. Allow to dry thoroughly.

Attach the angel's legs to her body with wire, connecting the loops in the back.

Attach angel to the stake with small nails, or drill a hole on each shoulder and make a large wire loop for hanging.

With a hot-glue gun or waterproof glue, glue

Supplies needed

piece of 1"x10" pine, 10" long

1"x2" stake, 24" long

tracing paper (or carbon paper) and pattern

sandpaper

drill with small, 1/8" bit

wire — 18-gauge is a good thickness

twine

Spanish moss

grapevine or other type vine

hot-glue gun and/or staple gun

matte spray paint

raffia

small, straw doll-hat

jig saw, scroll saw, or coping saw

acrylic paints

hammer and small nails

Spanish moss on the head for hair and a tiny bit on the birdhouse to simulate a nest.

Thread the birdhouse on a piece of twine and glue to her hand, or attach with a tiny nail. Glue hat on the angel's head.

Form wings by making a double loop of grapevine or other vine. (See the section on making a vine wreath for other vines easy to find and use.) You may use fresh vines, as they will dry in shape. Tie the center of the vine loops tightly with a small piece of twine and staple and/or hot-glue the wings to the center of the angel's back.

Make a bow of raffia and glue it to the center of the wings in back.

"Plant Kindness — Gather Love" Plaque

Supplies needed

Piece of scrap board
wire
raffia for bow
acrylic paints
drill

To compliment your gardening angel, make a plaque to hang near her on a fence post or on a wall near your indoor garden. Lorraine has become an expert at recycling scrap materials into something lovely.

Drill holes in the top of your signboard and make a wire hanger.

Paint the front of the plaque with white for a base coat.

Paint flowers in the center of the plaque according to the design. Letter the slogan.

Dip an old toothbrush into some thinned green paint and use your fingers to flip "spatters" onto the board. You may want to practice this part on a paper bag first to get the hang of the "spattering." Be certain to do this part outside; it's messy.

When the paint has dried, coat the plaque with matte finish or clear acrylic spray. Tie a raffia bow on the wire hanger.

Supplies needed

dried corn-cob and husks
acrylic paints and brush
hot-glue gun
dried moss and flowers

Corn-Cob Angel

If you live in the country, you can obtain a dried corn-cob and shucks straight from the field. City dwellers can buy fresh corn on the cob and enjoy eating it first. Save the husks when you shuck the corn.

After eating, take the cobs and wash them in

soapy water. Use a vegetable peeler or knife to scrape off the last remainders of corn. Let the cobs dry naturally in the sun or bake them in a very slow oven until thoroughly dry.

With your thumb, press down a spot near the top of the cob, making it as flat as possible in an oval shape. Using flesh-colored acrylic paint, paint an oval for the angel's face. Allow the paint to dry thoroughly.

Paint eyes white with a black or blue center; a red dot forms the mouth. Glue on moss for hair.

Carefully cut wings from dried corn-husks and glue in center of back. Form a halo by making a small wreath of raffia. Glue small dried flowers and leaves to form angel's bouquet.

Glue a loop of string in center of wings to hang angel, or run a stiff piece of wire into the center bottom of cob if you want the angel to accent a potted plant.

Gardening Angel

"Gather Love" Plaque

Corn-Cob Angels

Saintly Gardens

St. Fiacre, Patron of Gardeners

In spite of the abundance of statues of St. Francis seen in American gardens, the patron of gardeners is St. Fiacre (or Fiachra), a seventh-century hermit-priest and a hotheaded Irishman.

Once when Fiacre went to see a French bishop, his reputation for impatience preceded him, so the bishop kept him sitting on a rock in the garden all day to teach him a lesson. Apparently he spent the time in devotions; at any rate, after Fiacre's death, the rock was soon discovered to have miraculous powers. The king, sitting where Fiacre had waited for the bishop, was cured of an illness. The news spread quickly, and the place became a shrine.

Because of the number of pilgrims passing through Paris on their way to the shrine of St. Fiacre, an enterprising Parisian put up a tavern, calling it the Hotel de St. Fiacre. Soon there was a thriving cab business going between the hotel and the shrine. The cabs became known as *fiacres*, and St. Fiacre, by extension, became patron of cabdrivers.

Little is known for certain of the origins of this saint. His original Irish name may have been Fiachra. It is said that he was born in Ireland about the year 600 and raised in a monastery. Here he learned a deep love of silence, the joys of planting and harvesting crops, and an appreciation of nature. Drawn to the religious life and the desire to serve God in solitude, after he was ordained a priest, he established a hermitage near the Nore River. The name of the area — Kilfiachra — preserves his memory. Because of his herbal knowledge, people began to come to him for prayers, food, and healing.

Many of the Irish monks of this time period were sent out to Europe to spread the word of God. Fiacre went to France, where he was kindly received at Meaux by St. Faro, who gave him a piece of land on which to build a hermitage. He built his hut and began a garden and, as all good gardens do, his garden began to grow. He needed more space. Legend attributes a miracle in regard to the additional acreage. The bishop told Fiacre he could have as much land as he could entrench in one day. The story holds that he merely dragged his spade across the ground, causing trees to topple and bushes to be uprooted. Word of the miracle began to spread and again the poor and the sick began to flock to the humble monk.

Fiacre built an oratory which he dedicated to Our Lady, and, later, a hospice for travelers. He spent his time in prayer, working with his hands, and caring for the travelers and the poor of the area. Disciples gathered around him and they soon founded a monastery.

There is a legend that because of an incident with a meddlesome woman, who spoke against him to St. Faro, all women were excluded from his enclosure. There are many stories of misfortune which befell women who trespassed, even after his death. In reality, the exclusion of women was a common rule in the Irish foundations.

Fiacre's fame for miracles was widespread. All manner of diseases were cured by his touch — blindness, fevers, and especially tumors. After his death for many centuries, his chapel and his shrine drew the sick, and his intercession was especially sought after by persons suffering from hemorrhoids.

After his death August 18, 670, he was buried at his church at Breuil, where the fame of his sanctity soon spread because of the miracles wrought at his tomb. In 1568, the relics were removed to the cathedral at Meaux.

Fiacre is looked on as the patron saint of gardeners because of the fine vegetables he grew around his hermitage. The feast of St. Fiacre is September 1. Recognized in Europe since the Middle Ages, the saint's day has been celebrated with special Masses, floral processions, and pilgrimages. At one time in France, special floats with elaborate flower decorations paraded down streets strewn with flower petals. Special hymns in his honor were part of the celebrations in Ireland. His feast is not officially celebrated in the United States, although in recent years his story has begun to be better known here and occasionally garden statues of the saint are found in nurseries and garden-supply shops. His emblem in art is a spade.

Personalize a Spade

Personalize a trowel or spade as a special gift for your favorite gardener, or mark your own.

As I child, I remembered making woodburned projects with my brother's

Supplies needed

a candle in a safe container (or use the flame of a gas stove)

an ice pick

wooden-handled trowel or spade (natural finish; not painted)

large screw and hammer — optional

liquid brown shoe polish — optional

woodburning tool. Unfortunately I don't have one today, so my friend LaNell showed me how they used to make decorative "branded" projects in the country when she was a child.

Directions

With pencil, mark the name you want to "brand" on the wooden handle of your trowel or spade. Make the letters as squared-off as possible, as curved lines are difficult.

Hold the tip of the ice pick in the candle flame (or the flame from a gas stove) until the tip is red hot. Quickly lay it along one of the lines of your design and press to burn or brand that part of the line. Repeat until your entire design has been branded.

Wipe away the excess soot with a paper towel; the lines you have branded will retain a darker color than the wooden handle.

To make a simple decoration at each end of the name, turn a screw on its side and bang it with a hammer. This will leave a series of small lines cut into the wood.

Paint across the screw marks and over the name with brown shoe polish. Quickly wipe the excess shoe polish off. Brown polish will be left in the indentations from the screw and from your burning, and will also highlight and give an antiqued finish to the wooden handle.

Supplies needed

pair of plain cotton gardening gloves, off-white with no design

fabric markers

Green-Finger Gloves

This is a good project for younger school-aged children. Their original art enhances the practicality of a pair of gardening gloves.

If you can't obtain fabric markers, you can substitute permanent markers. There are sets of colorful markers, however, made especially for decorating fabric which you can purchase at an arts-and-craft store and at many fabric stores.

Have the children color the nail area of each finger of the glove green. Then have them draw a stem up each finger and put a flower at the top of each stem. Then they can add leaves and, possibly, a worm or butterfly to finish the project. Who needs a green thumb if you have eight green fingers?

Garden Row Markers

Supplies needed

plastic clothespins

plastic knives

hot-glue gun

Out in the country, after a garden is planted, most gardeners like to keep the seed packet at the end of the row until the plants get a good start, to remind themselves where they have planted what. A handy way to keep the packets in place is to make a set of garden row markers. If you don't have a large garden, you can use the markers to show what you have planted in your flower pots.

Directions

Apply hot glue to the top of the handle of a plastic knife; the stripe of glue should extend from the top of the handle about 1½". Attach a plastic

Garden Row Markers, left; Green-Finger Gloves, below

clothespin to the knife handle by setting 1½" of one of the sides of the clip in the glue. When the glue has hardened, you can grip a flower packet with the clip and stick the knife blade in the ground to mark your rows.

Other Garden Patrons

Although Fiacre is the best-known patron of gardeners, a number of other saints traditionally share the honor of this patronage. Images or other reminders of each are appropriate in today's garden. Although these saints all lived so far back in history that the stories of them have been embroidered during the centuries, we can recall that each of them, in their own day, was held up for honor by their peers as examples of saintly living. Faith, humility, and prayerfulness are virtues shared by all these gardening patrons, as well as their connection with the garden.

Adelard

St. Adelard (Adalhard), born in 753, was the grandson of Charles Martel. He became a monk at Corbie, Picardy, in 773. Here, his first assignment was as gardener of the monastery. He did his work humbly and piously, praying throughout the day. His great virtues eventually helped him to become abbot. Although he preferred the life of the monastery, Adelard was brought to court by his cousin Charlemagne, and became one of his advisers and chief minister to Charlemagne's oldest son, Pepin. After Pepin's death in 810, Adelard was named tutor of Pepin's son Benard. When he was accused of supporting a revolt against the Emperor Louis the Debonair, Adelard was exiled for five years until Louis decided he was innocent and recalled him to court. He was banished again in 821 to Corbie, where his reputation for holiness, austerity, and concern for the poor and the sick soon spread. He established another monastery, Corvey in Paderborn, and made both monasteries centers of learning and teaching both in Latin and the vernacular of German and French. He died at Corbie in 827.

Dorothy

According to tradition, Dorothy (Dorothea) was a resident of Caesarea, Cappadocia, martyred February 6, 311. She refused to sacrifice to the gods during Emperor Diocletian's persecution of the Christians. Two apostate women were sent to pervert her, but she re-converted them. She was taken before the prefect Sapricius, tried, tortured, and sentenced to be beheaded.

On the way to the place of execution, she met a young pagan lawyer named Theophilus. Mockingly, he said to her, "Bride of Christ, send me some fruits from your bridegroom's garden." Later versions of the legend have Dorothy sending him a basket of roses and apples by an angelic messenger, along with the message to meet her in the garden. The oldest version, however, tells that when her headdress was removed prior to her execution, she had it sent to the lawyer by a young boy. He found it filled with a heavenly fragrance of roses and fruits, and was himself converted to Christianity and martyred.

In art, Dorothy is represented with an angel and a wreath of flowers, or a basket of roses and fruit. She was regarded as the patroness of gardeners. Trees were blessed in her name on her feast day in some parts of Europe. She has been venerated in the Western Church since the seventh century.

Gertrude of Nivelles

St. Gertrude was born at Landen in 626. Both her parents, Blessed Pepin of Landen and Blessed Itta, were revered for their holy lives, and her sister Begga is also numbered among the saints.

According to her legend, at the age of ten she rejected the offer of marriage from the Merovingian king Dagobert I. She told him that she would marry no man, and that Christ alone would be her bridegroom.

In 640, on the death of her husband, Itta founded a double monastery (one for men and one for women) at Nivelles, and appointed Gertrude its abbess when she was judged old enough. Although she was still young, she carried out her responsibilities well with her mother's help. She gave encouragement and help to monks, particularly the Irish ones, to do missionary work in the neighborhood. She gave St. Foillan land and horses to enable him to found a monastery in the area.

At the age of 30, she resigned her office to her niece, and spent the rest of her life studying Scripture and doing penance. She was gifted with many visions. She died on March 17, 659, at the age of 33. Her cultus became widely spread in the Lowlands and neighboring countries, and a considerable body of folklore gathered round her name.

Gertrude's feast day in March is associated with the beginning of the new gardening season, and this is the source of her patronage of gardeners. Her iconography, however, cannot be explained so easily. In art, Gertrude is shown with a pastoral staff with a mouse running up it. She has traditionally been invoked against mice and rats. As late as the mid-nineteenth century, offerings of gold and silver mice were presented at her shrine in Cologne to secure her intercessory help with an infestation of the rodents. One possible explanation for this odd association, which seems to bear no relevance to any events in her life, may be the fact that her feast-day tended to coincide with the time of year that field mice awoke from hibernation and began to become a nuisance.

Phocas the Gardener

There was an early martyr, dates unknown, named Phocas, who suffered at Sinope in Pontus, on the southern shore of the Black Sea. It is known that a Christian community existed in the area from the first half of the second century. A sanctuary dedicated to Phocas was established here, and he was widely venerated by the first part of the fifth century when he was the subject of a panagyric preached by an early fifth-century bishop.

A gardener (and possibly a bishop) at Sinope, Paphlagonia, Phocas lived as an anchorite, pursuing an austere life of prayer and contemplation, offering shelter to travelers, and suffering martyrdom for his Faith. According to legend, he was denounced as a Christian and sentenced to death. When a squad of soldiers arrived at his house, he gave them shelter. When the soldiers told him they were seeking one Phocas, he told them he would tell them where to find Phocas in the morning, and encouraged them to rest. After preparing his soul for death, he dug his own grave. The next morning, when Phocas told the soldiers who he was, the soldiers were overcome by his courage and his kindness. They hesitated, but at his urging they beheaded him.

Tryphon

In the Latin Church, St. Tryphon's feast was observed along with two other early martyrs, Respicius and Nympha. He is greatly venerated in the Greek Church, and in this Church he is also the patron saint of gardeners. Many churches were dedicated to him, and Emperor Leo VI the Philosopher delivered a eulogy about him in the eighth century. The monk Theodoric of Fleury wrote an account of his life in the eleventh century which was based on earlier written legends. In Theodoric's story, Tryphon and Respicius were companions and their relics, along with those of a holy virgin named Nympha, were preserved at the Hospital of the Holy Ghost in Sassia. In 1566, the relics of these saints were transferred by Pope Pius V to the Church of St. Augustine.

Tryphon was said to have been born at Kampsade in Phyrgia, and as a boy took care of geese. During the Decian persecution, he was taken to Nicea about the year 250 and put to death in a horrible manner after he had converted the heathen prefect Licius. Fabulous stories are interwoven with his legend.

Make a Vine Wreath

Cut your vines in the yard or in a nearby woodsy area. Honeysuckle, grape, wisteria, and trumpet vines are all popular and easy to use. Almost any vine with a woody stem will do. Make certain you know which type of vine you are cutting; some vines, like poison ivy, can give you a rude rash! Cut lengths as long as possible, at least 3'. Strip the leaves from the vine. If you are not going to work with the vines immediately, put them in a bucket of water.

Supplies needed

fresh-cut vines about ⅛" thick

You can complete this project inside, but it is kind of messy, so it's a perfect project for a pleasant fall day outside.

Starting at the thickest end of your vine, gently bend the vine into a loop the approximate size you want your finished wreath to be. A wreath 9" to 12" in diameter is a good size to start with and makes a nice base for an herb wreath. A good size for a flower or harvest wreath is 12" to 15".

Holding the end of the loop in your left hand, begin twisting the loose end of the vine around the loop. When you run out of vine on that piece, take the thick end of a second piece, and holding it at the place where you started your first loop, wrap it around the loop. As you come to the end of each piece, tuck it in between the previous pieces to secure.

Vine Wreaths

Continue wrapping until your wreath is as thick as you want to make it. You can gently shape the wreath as you go if it is somewhat lopsided. The fresher and wetter the vine, the easier it will weave.

After your wreath is completed, hang it on a nail or hook outside to dry thoroughly. You will be surprised at the change in colors of some vines.

When your wreath is completely dry, at least two or three weeks, you can attach a small loop of wire on the back to hang it by. Now you are ready to decorate it.

Making the base for your wreath is easy and quick and costs nothing if you have a good supply of vines nearby. You may want to make several of these in different sizes to decorate for yourself or for a friend.

Make a Wind Sock

Wind socks were once reserved to airports as directional tools. Today, they are popular as a bright accent, hanging from a tree in the garden, although few gardeners really need to know the direction of the wind. Most of the ones we have seen in the store are very pricey. We made our own from inexpensive ribbon and a plastic soda bottle.

With the point of your scissors, or with a sharp knife, make a hole near the top of the soda bottle to allow you to get the scissors' point in.

Cut the top off the bottle.

Make another hole about 2" from the top of your first cut and cut off the bottom, leaving you with a 2"-wide band, or circlet, of plastic. Trim the edges as neatly as possible.

With a hole punch, punch two holes across from each other about ½" in from the top edge of your band.

Cut a piece of nylon twine or cord about 15" long and tie each end through one of the holes, making a knot so it won't slip. With nylon cord, you will need to burn the ends so that they won't fray. Do this carefully with a cigarette lighter or match. If a child is making this project, the parents need to help with this part.

Supplies needed

scissors

glue gun

hole punch

cigarette lighter or matches

wooden clothespin

9 strips of 1½" wide florist ribbon, each strip 24" long (This is a total of 18 feet, or 6 yards. The more colorful the better.)

empty plastic soda bottle

nylon twine

3 to 5 small silk flowers, optional

Windsock

Also, glue guns can be dangerous! Parental supervision will be necessary.

Make a fold 2½" to 3" from the top of one strip of ribbon.

Fold the ribbon over the top of the band with the short end to the inside. Put a thin line of glue across the bottom of the short end. Using your clothespin, press the glued end of the ribbon to attach it to the long side of the ribbon, making a loop across the plastic band. Using the clothespin will keep you from burning your fingers.

Continue making ribbon loops over the band until the entire band is covered. Try to avoid getting any glue on the plastic as it will cause the plastic to melt.

When all your ribbon is attached, you can glue on a few flowers if you like. The flowers can be glued to the ribbon at the part where it covers the band. Hang your wind sock outside from a tree in the garden for a colorful accent.

*Florist ribbon is available from most arts and crafts stores. Or, if you want a multi-colored windsock and don't want to buy several rolls of ribbon, you may find a friendly florist willing to sell you the yardage you need at an inexpensive price.

Mini Yule-Log

A miniature yule-log makes a nice table decoration at the Christmas season. Throw it in the fireplace at the end of the season for one last burst of fragrance.

Supplies needed

piece of dried tree branch about 12" long and as thick as you can find to simulate a log

dried cones or nuts

greenery; fir or short-leaf pine, or use rosemary sprigs and bay leaves for a delicious smell

candle stubs or paraffin (at the jelly-making supplies section of the grocery store)

empty coffee can

paper ribbon (optional)

Mini Yule Log

Cover your counter or table with several layers of paper for protection as you work. If your "log" is dirty, rinse it off and allow to dry thoroughly before beginning work.

Melt your wax in the bottom of an old coffee can on the lowest setting of your stove. It is safest to put the can in a pan of water, making a homemade double boiler. Always keep a box of baking soda on hand to put out a paraffin fire; should the wax spill and flame up, throw the soda over it to put out the fire. It's messy, but safety first! This part of the project is dangerous and should always be supervised by an adult if children are involved.

Carefully spoon the hot wax on the top of the log, adding your greenery and pressing it into the wax to hold. Work on a single area at a time until your design is complete.

When the wax dries, it will hold your greenery and dried materials to the log.

St. Thérèse of Lisieux, Patron of Florists

Marie Françoise Thérèse Martin was the youngest child of Louis and Zelie Martin, a prosperous middle-class couple. A bright, affectionate child, she suffered a long period of melancholy and acute sensitivity after her mother's early death. In 1866, she experienced a sudden transformation which resulted in a new self-possession and maturity. Feeling drawn to the life of Carmel, she applied for admission at the age of 14. Initially she was denied because of her age, but after some difficulty she was allowed to enter on April 9, 1888, at the age of 15. She received the name Thérèse of the Child Jesus.

Here in the cloister of Lisieux, Thérèse spent the remaining years of her life. In 1896, Thérèse contracted tuberculosis and died on September 30, 1897. Before her death, at the bidding of her superiors, Thérèse wrote her autobiography in which she explained her spirituality, her "Little Way of Spiritual Childhood." This spirituality consists essentially in the cultivation of that childlike relationship with the Father taught by Jesus in the Gospels.

Her memoirs were gathered under the title *Story of a Soul,* and what began as a simple notification to the other Carmels eventually traveled around the world. Thérèse was beatified in 1923 and canonized in 1925.

Thérèse believed in living Faith to the fullest in every moment, regardless of which state of life a person was in. This required self-abandonment to God, acceptance of suffering, and attempting to live out Christian principals in simplicity and humility. When she was close to death, she told one of the sisters that she would spend her life in heaven doing good for those on earth. She also promised that after death a shower of roses would fall, bringing God's graces to many of the faithful. This gave rise to her nickname, the "Little Flower." Officially declared patroness of foreign missions, Thérèse is also considered patron of florists. Her symbol in art is a crucifix entwined with roses.

"Jesus deigned to teach me this mystery. He set before me the book of nature. I understood how all the flowers He has created are beautiful, how the splendor of the rose and the whiteness of the lily do not take away the perfume of the little violet or the delightful simplicity of the daisy. I understood that if all flowers wanted to be roses, nature would lose her springtime beauty, and the fields would no longer be decked out with little wild flowers.

"And so it is in the world of souls, Jesus' garden. He willed to create great souls comparable to lilies and roses, but He has created smaller ones and these must be content to be daisies or violets destined to give joy to God's glances when He looks down at His feet. Perfection consists in doing His will, in being what He wills us to be."

St. Thérèse of Lisieux

St. Francis of Assisi, Patron of Ecologists

No saint throughout history is better known for his love of all created things than the *poverello* (poor man) of Assisi, Francis Bernardone (c. 1181-1226). There is nothing more attractive than a happy person, and St. Francis was filled with joy. His love of God was a source of ecstatic joy, which is one of the characteristic marks of St. Francis and his followers. It is probably because of this contagious, unbounded joy that he has had such an appeal to all people throughout the centuries. More than an inspired individualist, the great founder of the Friars Minor was a man of tremendous spiritual insight and power, whose consuming love for Jesus Christ and redeemed creation found expression in all he said and did.

The son of a wealthy fabric merchant, at about the age of 20, after a period of captivity by enemies of Assisi and an illness, Francis began to find more serious things on his mind than the amusements common to his class. Praying in the church of San Damiano one day, he heard the image on a crucifix speak to him: "Go, Francis, and repair my house, which as you see is falling into ruin." Taking the words literally, Francis sold some of his father's goods and used the money to repair the church. Because of this, his father disinherited and disowned him. Willingly giving up all claim to worldly goods, Francis went to live in a shack, spending his time among the poor and the sick. His happy nature remained with him and attracted many people. Some of his youthful friends joined him in his poverty, and in preaching. In 1210, this group obtained the blessing of Pope Innocent III, marking the beginning of the Franciscan order, which spread rapidly all over the world. In 1224, Francis mystically received the sacred stigmata, the wounds of the Passion of Christ. To date, science still has no explanation of these marks. Francis died in Assisi in 1226 at the age of 44.

St. Francis is one of the most popular saints of all times. His image is found in gardens throughout the world, probably because of his great love of created things. Francis is the patron of merchants, of Italy, and of Catholic Action. He was a legendary champion of snared birds, beaten horses, and hungry dogs. In our own times, Pope John Paul II named him patron saint of ecologists. He is invoked for the love of all persons and for help when one is bored. The next time you have that restless "what do I do now" feeling, ask St. Francis to help you find something interesting to do!

The Little Flowers of St. Francis

In the fourteenth century, a delightful book entitled *Fioretti di San Francesco*, or *The Little Flowers of St. Francis*, appeared. It is primarily an Italian translation of an earlier Latin work which was written between 1322 and 1328. The authorship of either the original or the translation is not authoritatively known, but the book became a treasure of Italian literature and led to much of the great popularity of Francis among the ordinary people of Europe. In the Middle Ages, *Fioretti*, literally translated "little flowers," was a generic term that meant a collection or anthology. ("Anthology" in English literally signifies "to gather flowers.") Whether the title was a studied one or merely a happy accident, the title captures the spirit and the tone of the stories which are the oral traditions of the early days, preserved and written down by the Friars of the Marches of Ancona. Not a biography or a life of the saint, the *Little Flowers* are a collection of simple stories about him and his companions which bring to life the spirit, winsomeness, and simplicity of the early Franciscans.

Brother Sun, Sister Moon

Francis, wholly wrapped up in the love of God, discerned perfectly the goodness of God in every creature. Because of this, he had a singular and intimate love of creatures, especially of those in which was figured anything pertaining to God or the Order.

Francis especially loved the Christmas season. He admonished the farmers to give their stock extra corn and hay at Christmas "for reverence of the Son of God whom, on such a night the blessed Virgin Mary did lay down in the stall between the ox and the ass." Believing that all creation should rejoice at Christmas, he knew that the dumb creatures had no other means of doing so except by enjoying more comfort and better food. He also asked people to throw out grain to feed the wild birds, and to be especially generous to the poor at this time of year.

For Francis, sadness and moroseness were signs of hypocrisy and sin — a person who is sad must be in sin. "It is not fitting," he said, "that a servant of God should offer to men the spectacle of sadness and trouble, but rather one of constant cheerfulness." He did not confuse sadness with suffering, however, and felt that suffering could be a source of joy if it helped to conform one to Christ.

Francis felt that idleness led to a person's becoming lukewarm in his devotion, and wanted all his friars to labor and be exercised humbly in good works in order that they be less burdensome to men and that "neither heart nor tongue may wander in ease. Let those who know nothing learn to work." Once, when Francis was cultivating his garden, a brother asked him, "Francis, what would you do if you learned you were to die tomorrow?" The saint replied, "I would keep on cultivating my garden."

Francis gave instructions to the brother who did the garden not to plant the entire garden in pot herbs (food and useful herbs), but to leave some part of it to produce green herbs (flowers), which in their time should produce flowers for the friars, for the love of Him Who is called the "flower of the field" and the "lily of the valley." Francis told him to make a "fair pleasaunce" in some part of the garden, planting there all sweet-smelling herbs and all herbs which bring forth fair flowers, that in their time they might call them that looked upon those herbs and flowers to the praise of God. Francis told his friars, "Every creature cries aloud 'God made me for thee,' man!' "

The friars who lived with Francis testified that they saw him rejoice, within and without, in all things created, so that when touching or seeing them his spirit seemed to be not on earth but in heaven. It did not seem strange to these friars that fire, water, and other creatures without reason were obedient to Francis and venerated him because these created things drew him so close to God.

For most of the last part of his life, Francis was afflicted with a condition that caused great pain in his eyes and eventually this condition, or the treatments for it, blinded him. Two years before his death, he was staying in a small cell of reeds near St. Damian, and the infirmity in his eyes caused him to be temporarily blinded for more than two months. So many mice came into his cell and worried him that he had no peace and could not even pray. When he attempted to eat, the mice overran his food and worried him very much. It seemed, both to himself and to his fellows, that this was a diabolical temptation. At last, he prayed fervently to God that he be allowed to bear this patiently. Interiorly, God asked him, if he knew that in exchange for these infirmities he would receive a treasure greater than the entire earth, would he not rejoice? Francis contemplated on this and the next day told his companions, "If an emperor should give to a slave his entire kingdom, should not the slave rejoice? " Then, telling them that he wished to make a new praise of the creatures of the Lord which we daily use and without which we cannot live, and in whom the human race much offends their Creator, and because we are continually ungrateful for so much, not praising God, the Creator and Giver of all things as we ought, Francis sat down and composed a song, teaching his fellows to say and sing it. Francis asked the brothers to sing this song in the countryside as minstrels, asking to be paid, as minstrels were paid. Instead of asking for money, however, the brothers were to ask to be paid in repentance. When Francis heard that the Bishop and the Podesta (mayor) of Assisi were in disagreement, he amended his verse to include a praise of those who pardon for God's sake. He commanded one of the brothers to call the Bishop and the Podesta together and sing the canticle (song). This was done, and the two who were at war made peace.

This is the song of praise that St. Francis composed:

The Canticle of the Sun

Most high, omnipotent, good Lord,
Praise, glory, and benediction, all are Thine.
To Thee alone do they belong, Most High,
And there is no man fit to mention Thee.
Praise be to Thee, my Lord, with all Thy creatures,
Especially to my worshipful brother sun,
The which lights up the day, and through him dost
Thou brightness give;
And beautiful is he and radiant with splendor great;
Of Thee, Most High, signification gives.
Praised be my Lord, for sister moon and for the stars,
In Heaven Thou hast formed them clear and precious and fair.
Praised be my Lord for brother wind,
And for the air and clouds and fair and every kind of
    weather,
By the which Thou givest to Thy creatures nourishment.
Praised by my Lord for sister water,
The which is greatly helpful and humble and precious and pure.
Praised be my Lord for brother fire,
By the which Thou lightest up the dark,
And fair is he and gay and mighty and strong.
Praised be my Lord for our sister, mother earth,
The which sustains and keeps us
And brings forth divers fruits with grass and flowers bright.
Praised be my Lord for those who for Thy love forgive,
And weakness bear and tribulation.
Blessed those who shall in peace endure,
For by Thee, Most High, shall they be crowned.
Praised be my Lord for our sister, the bodily death,

From the which no living man can flee.
Woe to them who die in mortal sin,
Blessed those who shall find themselves in Thy most holy will,
For the second death shall do them no ill.
Praise ye and bless ye my Lord and give Him thanks,
And be subject unto Him with great humility.

Isidore the Farmer

Isidore was born at Madrid (c. 1070) and spent his entire life in the service of the same employer, John de Vergas, working as a laborer on his farm at Torrelaguna.

Isidore married a woman as poor, and as good, as he was. After the death of their only child, the couple vowed to serve God in celibacy. His legend contains many miraculous events. Wanting to attend Mass before work each day, he arrived late, and one of his fellow workers complained. When his master went to speak to Isidore about this, he found that angels were helping Isidore plow, so that he was actually completing the work of more than a single laborer.

He is also said to have brought his master's dead daughter back to life, and to have caused a spring to burst from the dry, barren land. One story, which illustrates his love of animals, says that while taking a sack of corn to be ground one cold winter's day, he saw a number of birds perched disconsolately on the bare branches, unable to find anything to eat. In spite of the ridicule of his companion, Isidore opened the sack and poured half the grain out for the birds to eat. The companion was surprised on arrival at the mill to find that the sack was full and the corn, when ground, produced double the normal amount of flour.

If the stories of Isidore have been delicately embroidered, it is still clear that he was a model worker, a kind neighbor, and a devout Christian. His life became a model of Christian perfection lived in the world. During each work day he prayed faithfully, and communicated with his guardian angel and with the saints. In addition to his miracles, Isidore was known for his piety and his charity to the poor. His wife, Maria Torribia, resembled him in character, and she is also considered a saint in Spain. Isidore died on May 15, 1130. Forty years after his death, Isidore's body was transferred to a more honorable shrine, from the cemetery to the church of St. Andrew, and his cult began to spread with the report of many miracles and favors attributed to his intercession.

In 1211 he is said to have appeared in a vision to the King of Castile, who was then fighting the Moors in the pass of Navas de Tolosa. The saint showed King Alphonse an unknown path by means of which he was able to surprise and defeat the enemy. King Philip III attributed his own recovery from a serious illness to Isidore's intercession.

The Spanish royal family had long desired to have St. Isidore formally enrolled among the saints and he was canonized in 1622. In art, St. Isidore's emblem is a sickle or a plow.

St. John Gualbert, Patron of Forest Workers

St. John Gualbert was born at Florence towards the end of the tenth century, the son of a nobleman. After his older brother was killed by a man reputed to be his friend, John determined to avenge him. Coming upon the murderer one day in a narrow passage, John drew his sword and advanced upon the defenseless man, who fell to his knees with his arms crossed on his breast. Suddenly the young man's heart was seized with the remembrance of Christ, who prayed for His murderers on the cross. John put up his sword and embraced his enemy with forgiveness, parting from him in peace.

This proved to be a turning point in John's life. From this encounter, John went to the monastery of San Miniato, where he offered his prayers before the crucifix in the church. As he was praying, the crucifix miraculously seemed to bow its head in a token of the acceptance of John's sacrifice of his revenge and his sincere repentance. Divine grace took possession of him and he asked the abbot to be admitted to the religious life. At first, fearing John's father, the abbot would not allow it. After a few days, John cut his hair himself, borrowed a habit, and devoted himself in such disposition of a true penitent that the abbot conceded and accepted him.

Later, seeking a closer solitude, John and one companion went to Fiesole, where they built a monastery of timber and mud and began a community according to the primitive and austere rule and spirit of St. Benedict. The Vallumbrosans, as his followers came to be called, stressed charity and poverty and admitted lay brothers, an innovation for religious congregations at the time.

John became known for his aid to the poor, his fierce opposition to simony, his miracles, gift of prophecy, and spiritual wisdom, which attracted great crowds who came to seek his advice. The order spread throughout Italy. John died near Florence on July 12, 1073, and was canonized in 1193.

Supplies needed

brown paper sacks

leftover pictorial calendar (we used a Victorian cat calendar) or attractive magazine cover

white craft-glue

scissors, including pinking shears if you have them

stainless steel or other metal cooking-bowls

warm water

oven

Paper Bowls

An inexpensive yet lovely way to present your gift of potpourri, scented cones, or homemade treats is to craft your own paper bowls. The cost of paper, a wood-based product, is at an all-time high due to previous poor forestry management, and the new regulations intended to correct these practices. We can and should recycle and re-use paper ourselves; this is one decorative way to do so.

Directions

Fill your sink about 6" deep with the hottest water from your tap.

Use a plate to trace a circle on a brown paper bag and cut it out with regular scissors. Trace the same plate onto the picture portion of a leftover calendar or decorative magazine cover. (Any picture on heavy clay-coated paper will work; thinner papers do not do as well.) Cut out your calendar page with pinking shears, if you have them; use regular scissors if you like.

Soak the two circles in the warm water for at least 10 minutes. When the paper is well-soaked, place the brown paper on the counter and gently smooth most of the water off with your hand.

Pour on about 1 to 2 tsps. of white craft-glue and smooth it across the paper with your hand, making certain to spread the glue clear to the edge of the circle. The glue will thin with the water; don't worry, it doesn't take much.

Next place your picture circle on top of the brown paper one. Gently smooth the two pages together.

Carefully lay the wet paper in a metal bowl. One with sloping sides makes a wider dish; one with straight up-and-down sides makes a tighter bowl. Carefully press the paper into the bowl you are using for a mold. Use your fingers to arrange and drape the sides to form a pretty shape.

Take the top rack out of your oven and pre-heat the oven to 200°. Place your paper bowl in the metal mold into the oven. After about ten minutes, check to make certain the paper is not sticking to the metal bowl; if so, carefully peel it loose and let it remain loosely in the metal bowl until it is nearly dry. Check every ten minutes or so, and when your paper bowl is dry enough to hold its shape, remove it from the mold and let it dry another few minutes until it is completely dry.

Our calendar had earth tones, so the brown paper made a beautiful backing. If you prefer, you can use one of the cheapest paper plates for the back; soak as you did the brown paper. Experiment with other metal bakeware for a variety of shapes.

Scented Pine Cones

Clean your cones if they are not already clean. You can put them in a plastic clothes-basket and shoot the hose on them outside; let them dry thoroughly. Some cones, when wet, will close up; they will open again when they are completely dry.

Pour half your potpourri oil and an ounce of almond oil in the shot glass. If the oils do not mix well, you will need to stir them each time you dip up some.

Cover your workspace with newspaper covered with waxed paper, or work over a plastic-topped area; oils can damage wood and painted surfaces.

Cut your straw in half. You will use a piece to carry the oil to the cones. A medicine dropper is easier, but many households do not have a spare.

> **Supplies needed**
>
> 8 oz. bottle spicy potpourri oil
>
> 2 oz. almond oil
>
> 1 sack clean pine, fir, or other cones
>
> plastic soda straw or medicine dropper
>
> small glass such as a shot glass
>
> large glass or ceramic bowl

Holding the cone upright over the glass bowl, dip your straw into the oil. Put your finger securely over the top of the straw and this will hold some oil in the straw. Hold the filled straw over the top of the cone and release your finger; the oil will drip down onto the cone. Set the cone carefully in the bowl.

Continue scenting all the cones, carefully placing each one upright in the bowl. Stack a second layer on top of the first, etc. When all cones have been scented, you can drizzle the remaining oil over the top of the stack.

Leave cones sitting overnight so that all the oil will be taken up. Seal completed cones in zip-lock bags until ready for use.

St. Rita of Cascia, Saint of the Impossible

Rita was born near Spoleto, Italy, in 1381. Although she wanted to become a nun, her parents wished her to marry at a young age, and she acquiesced. She married at the age of 12, had two sons, and was widowed 18 years later. Rita's marriage was an unhappy one. Her husband was abusive and often mistreated her, but her patience and continual prayers for him eventually won a change of heart from him. For a short time before his politically motivated assassination, the household was a happy one. When Rita's two sons vowed to avenge their father's death, and when her pleading could not change their intentions, the saint prayed that they would die before committing such a dreadful crime. Both died with the consolations of the Church, forgiving their father's murderers.

Rita applied for admittance into the convent of the Augustinians in Cascia, but her admittance was denied three times because of stipulations in the rules, which barred acceptance of widows. Her prayers were answered when her patron saints appeared to her one night and led her through locked and barred doors into the chapel of the convent, where the astonished sisters discovered her the next morning. Seeing this unusual entry as an indication of the will of God, Rita was at last admitted to the convent, where she became known for her austerity in penance, prayerful disposition, and deep love and concern for others.

In 1441, after hearing a moving sermon about the crown of thorns, Rita begged Our Lord to be allowed to share in some way in His Passion, and received a thorn wound on her forehead. This wound festered and produced an offensive odor, and the saint spent the next 15 years of her life in reverential seclusion, a victim soul.

Rita died in 1457 at the age of 76. The cell where her body lay was filled with an extraordinary perfume, and a light emanated from the wound on her forehead.

Because of her reputation for holiness and the sweet perfume that continued to emanate from the wooden casket, it was placed in a spot where the cloistered nuns and the many pilgrims could venerate its precious contents. The body was examined in 1627 prior to her beatification and found to be incorrupt. Numerous miracles and unusual happenings are related about the life of St. Rita. She was canonized in 1900.

The Bees of St. Rita

One curiosity in the life of this saint is the colony of bees which make their home at her convent.

When Rita was an infant, tiny white bees were once seen swarming about her mouth. This unusual incident is always mentioned in Rita's biographies and usually given a miraculous connotation, but they could as well have been attracted by something sweet she had eaten. About 200 years after her death, however, a strange variety of bees took up residence in an old wall of the monastery and have lived there continuously since that time. They remain in hibernation 10 months of the year and emerge during Holy Week. They have never been seen to leave the convent enclosure, and after a few weeks of activity about the gardens and rooms of the convent, they return to the ancient wall after the feast of St. Rita on May 22. There, they seal themselves into holes which they make themselves. The sisters of the convent do not consider their presence or behavior to be in any way of a miraculous nature. It is regarded as purely a natural phenomenon which, by an unusual coincidence, occurs in the walls of their convent.

Although the bees in St. Rita's life are not considered miraculous, the sight of any bee can remind us of this saint and her loving, prayerful patience, qualities any gardener needs.

Make a Bee House

All bees are a boon to gardeners for their work in pollinating fruits and flowers. There are a number of types of solitary bees who tunnel into dead or soft wood, such as mason bees, carpenters, leaf cutters, and cuckoo bees. Mason bees get their name from the variety that attaches its nest of mixed clay and saliva to stones or walls, and in some parts of the country are commonly called dirt daubers. Unlike honey bees and bumble bees, which live in colonies, the solitary bees live alone but often nest close together.

Supplies needed

8" piece of 4"x4" post or other
  type of fence post
saw
drill with 5/16" bit
glue gun
pieces of bark

You can make a simple bee house to encourage solitary bees to live, and work, in your flower garden. Mount the house on a post or a tree trunk or set it on a stump or rock in your garden or orchard.

Directions

Cut a slice off the top of the post to make a slant for the roof.

Drill 5/16" holes 1" apart on the front of the house, evenly spaced in rows of 3 across and 6 down. Make each hole about 1¼" deep.

Decide where you will place your house and select an appropriate manner of affixing it. You can nail it to a post to stand alone, drill a hole on the back to hang it on a nail on a fence, or drive a nail in the back and use wire to hang it in a tree.

Using a hot-glue gun, affix pieces of bark for the roof, overlapping from the front to the back. Allow the first row to extend about ½" over the front wall to help keep off the rain. Place the house in the garden and invite the bees to move in.

Beeswax Candles

Supplies needed

sheet beeswax, available from the arts and crafts store

candle wick

paper plate

microwave

lavender flowers — optional

fresh rosemary sprig — optional

raffia — optional

Handmade beeswax candles are simple to make and can impart a warm, comforting light to any room.

Carefully cut sheet beeswax into rectangles 8" by 7". Cut a piece of candle wick 8½" long for each candle.

Place 1 sheet of the beeswax on a paper plate and microwave it on high power for about 15 seconds.

Remove from microwave and lay a strip of wick along an 8" edge, leaving about ½" of the wick sticking above the wax. Carefully roll the wax around the wick about 2 turns.

At this point, you can sprinkle about 1 tsp. of chopped rosemary leaf or of dried lavender flowers on the rest of the sheet of wax.

Return the wax to the microwave for another 15 seconds. Remove from the oven and slide onto a flat surface.

Carefully roll the wax until all has been rolled into a candle shape. Press the top of the wax toward the wick to make it point slightly. Carefully run your finger down the outside edge to make certain it has sealed.

If you are planning on presenting some of your candles to a friend as a gift, you can tie several of them together with a thin strip of raffia. It may be a good idea to wrap a piece of paper around each candle, taping it shut, to protect the lovely shape of the wax until time to burn it.

Bee House

Beeswax Candles

Appendix

Pattern for Gardening Angel (see page 121)

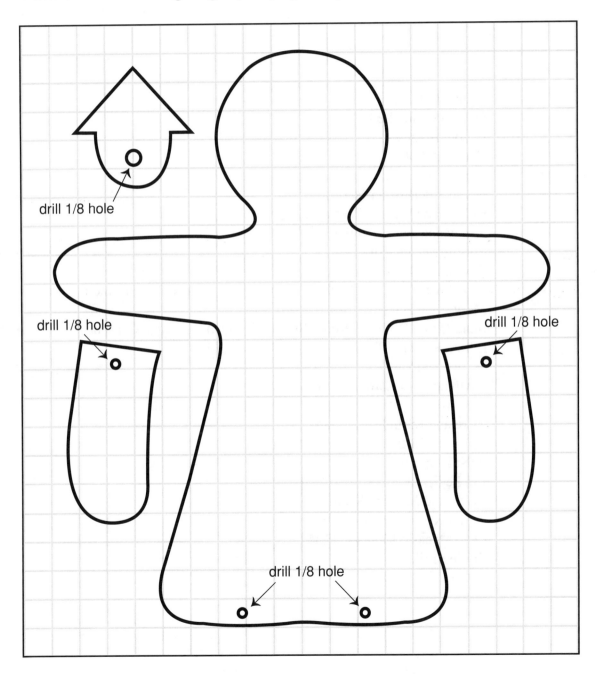

drill 1/8 hole

drill 1/8 hole

drill 1/8 hole

drill 1/8 hole

Thanks

Joanna Ball
Sam and Danielle Ball
Evelyn Blozek
Chuck Bolton
Ron Bujok
Glynn and Heather Burleson
Roland and Norma Contreras
Randy and Julie Douglas
Lorraine Featherston
Rev. James Gaunt, C.S.B.
Rev. Gustavo Guijarro-Montes, Shrine of the Holy Child of the Doves
Mary Ellen Hall
Irene Jacob, Director, Rodef Shalom Biblical Botanical Garden
Lillian Kaiser
Mary's Gardens
Lawrence and Carol LeLeux
Rev. Michael Miller, C.S.B.
Mike and Karin Murthough
Virginia Murthough
LaNell Orsack
Jim Pedicord
Curtis and Julianne Sandford
Father Kevin Shanley, O. Carm.
Rev. Atanasio Linh Vy, C.M.C.
Bea Whitfil

Selected Bibliography

Attwater, Donald. *The Avenel Dictionary of Saints.* New York: Avenel Books, 1981.

Ball, Ann. *Catholic Book of the Dead.* Huntington, Indiana: Our Sunday Visitor, 1995.

Ball, Ann. *A Handbook of Catholic Sacramentals.* Huntington, Indiana: Our Sunday Visitor, 1991.

Berrall, Julia S. *The Garden: An Illustrated History.* New York: The Viking Press, 1966.

Bogle, Joanna. *A Book of Feasts and Seasons.* Melksham, England: The Cromwell Press, 1992.

Bonaventure, Saint. *The Little Flowers of St. Francis.* New York: E. P. Dutton and Co., 1951.

Bremness, Lesley, ed. *Herbs.* Pleasantville, New York: The Reader's Digest Association, 1990

Castleman, Michael. "Herbs and the Healthy Heart." *The Herb Quarterly.* Boiling Spring, Pennsylvania: Long Mountain Press. Issue No. 57, Spring 93, p. 14.

Ciarrocchi, Maura. "Seeds of Faith." *Our Sunday Visitor.* Huntington, Indiana: Our Sunday Visitor Press, Inc., June 27, 1993, p.5.

Clarke, John, O.C.D., trans. *St. Thérèse of Lisieux: A Collection of Meditations.* Reno: Carmel of Reno, 1984

Cruz, Joan Carroll. *The Incorruptibles.* Rockford, Illinois: TAN Books, 1977.

Debelis, Inge N., project ed. *Magic and Medicine of Plants.* Pleasantville, New York: The Readers Digest Association, 1990.

Delaney, John J. *Dictionary of Saints*. Garden City, New York: Doubleday and Company, 1980.

Dues, Greg. *Catholic Customs and Traditions*. Mystic, Connecticut: Twenty-Third Publications, 1993.

Farb, Peter. *The Land, Wildlife, and Peoples of the Bible*. New York: Harper and Row, 1967.

Friedlander, Barbara. *Vegetables, Fruits, and Nuts*. New York: Grosset and Dunlap, 1974.

Freze, Michael, S.F.O. *Patron Saints*. Huntington, Indiana: Our Sunday Visitor, 1992.

Gaden, Eileen. *Biblical Garden Cookery*. Chappaqua, New York: Christian Herald Books, 1976.

Graham, Joe S., ed. *Hecho En Tejas: Texas-Mexican Folk Arts & Crafts*. Denton, Texas: University of North Texas Press, 1991.

Grieve, Mrs. M. *A Modern Herbal*. New York: Dover Publications, 1982.

Herbermann, Charles G. and collaborators, eds. *The Catholic Encyclopedia*. New York: The Encyclopedia Press, Inc., 1913 edition.

Hill, Madelene, Barclay, Gwen, and Hardy, Jean. *Southern Herb Growing*. Fredericksburg, Texas: Shearer Publishing, 1986

Hyanes, Edward. *A History of Gardens and Gardening*. New York: Praeger Publishing, 1971.

International Commission on English in the Liturgy. *The Book of Blessings*. New York: Catholic Book Publishing Co., 1989.

Jacob, Irene and Walter. "Rodef Shalom Biblical Garden." *The Herb Quarterly*. Fall, 1994, p. 26.

Lathrop, Norma Jean. *Herbs*. Tucson, Arizona: HPBooks, 1981.

Maus, Cynthia Pearl. *Christ and the Fine Arts*. New York: Harper and Brothers Publishers, 1938.

Needham, Bobbe. *Beastly Abodes*. New York: Sterling Publishing Co., 1995.

O'Connell, Rev. John P., ed. *The Holy Bible: Holy Trinity Edition*. Chicago: The Catholic Press, 1951.

Prenis, John. *Herb Grower's Guide*. Philadelphia: Running Press, 1986.

Stimpson, George. *A Book About a Thousand Things*. New York: Harper and Brothers, 1946.

Utterback, Christina. "Indigo: Mystic Blues." *The Herb Quarterly*. Boiling Springs, Pennsylvania: Long Mountain Press. Issue No. 52, Winter 91/92, p. 29.

Wagner, Kimberly J. "Gardening With the Bible." *Catholic Digest*. St. Paul, Minnesota: University of St Paul. May, 1992.

Walsh, Michael, ed. *Butler's Lives of the Saints: Concise Edition*. San Francisco: Harper and Row, 1985.

Weiser, Francis X. *Handbook of Christian Feasts and Customs*. New York: Harcourt, Brace & World, Inc., 1958.

Wittmann, Christine. "Rites of Spring." *The Herb Quarterly*. Boiling Springs, Pennsylvania: Long Mountain Press. Issue No. 53, Spring 92, p. 28.

Zeiller, Jacques. *Christian Beginnings*. New York: Hawthorne Books, 1960.

Sources

We hope you can easily find sources close to you for all materials and supplies needed to make the projects in this book. If not, the following sources have indicated a willingness to help you in locating supplies, or to provide them by mail.

A Moveable Feast, 2202 W. Alabama, Houston, TX 77098, has a large selection of materials for potpourri and essential oils. Write or call them at (713) 528-3585 to inquire about products and prices.

The Fitzgibbon Company, Catholic Religious Goods and Gift Store, 609 Fifth Street, Sioux City, IA 51101. Write or call them at 1-800-352-0033 to inquire about prices for religious goods.

American Gourd Society, P.O. Box 274-P, Mt. Gilead, OH 43338. Write them for helpful information about gourds.

Index

Our Sunday Visitor...

Your Source for Discovering the Riches of the Catholic Faith

Our Sunday Visitor has an extensive line of materials for young children, teens, and adults. Our books, Bibles, booklets, CD-ROMs, audios, and videos are available in bookstores worldwide.

To receive a FREE full-line catalog or for more information, call **Our Sunday Visitor** at **1-800-348-2440**. Or write, **Our Sunday Visitor** / 200 Noll Plaza / Huntington, IN 46750.

Please send me:__ A catalog
Please send me materials on:
   __ Apologetics and catechetics   __ Reference works
   __ Prayer books   __ Heritage and the saints
   __ The family   __ The parish

Name_____
Address_____Apt._____
City_____State ____Zip_____
Telephone (   ) _____

A73BBABP

Please send a friend:__ A catalog
Please send a friend materials on:
   __ Apologetics and catechetics   __ Reference works
   __ Prayer books   __ Heritage and the saints
   __ The family   __ The parish

Name_____
Address_____Apt._____
City_____State ____Zip_____
Telephone (   ) _____

A73BBABP

 Our Sunday Visitor
200 Noll Plaza
Huntington, IN 46750
1-800-348-2440
OSVSALES@AOL.COM

Your Source for Discovering the Riches of the Catholic Faith